I0014778

PYTHON FOR ACCOUNTING

Hayden Van Der Post

Reactive Publishing

To my daughter, may she know anything is possible.

CONTENTS

INTRODUCTION

In today's rapidly evolving business landscape, the field of accounting is undergoing a profound transformation. No longer limited to ledger books and manual calculations, the accountant's toolkit has expanded to include powerful technological tools, and at the forefront of this revolution stands Python, a versatile and dynamic programming language. Welcome to "Python for Accounting," a book that bridges the traditional world of finance with the cutting-edge possibilities of automation and data analytics.

In an era where data is king, the ability to extract valuable insights from financial information is a skill in high demand. Imagine being able to automate tedious tasks, analyze complex financial data with ease, and gain deeper insights into your company's financial health through the power of Python. Whether you are a seasoned accountant looking to stay ahead in a competitive industry or a newcomer to the world of finance eager to harness the potential of technology, this book is your key to unlocking a world of new opportunities.

In the pages that follow, you will embark on a journey that will not only teach you the fundamentals of Python programming but also show you how to apply these skills directly to the realm of accounting. You will witness how Python can become your most valuable ally, helping you work more efficiently, make more informed financial decisions, and even develop innovative solutions to complex financial challenges.

Whether you're intrigued by the idea of automating repetitive tasks, intrigued by the potential of data-driven insights, or simply excited about the prospect of transforming the accounting profession with technology, "Python for Accounting" will serve as your trusty guide. As you delve into the world of Python programming, you'll discover that the possibilities are endless, and your journey begins right here, right now. So, let's embark on this exciting adventure and unlock the hidden potential of Python for accounting. Your financial future is just a few pages away.

Why Python for Accounting?

As you embark on your journey into the world of Python for accounting, it's essential to understand why this programming language has become an indispensable tool in the realm of finance and accounting. In this chapter, we'll explore the profound relevance of Python in accounting and unveil the numerous benefits it offers in managing financial data and tasks efficiently.

Python has established itself as a versatile and powerful language with applications spanning across various industries. However, it's not only about its versatility but also about its simplicity and ease of use that makes it an ideal choice for accountants. Python's readability and clean syntax make it a great language for those who may not have a strong programming background.

When we talk about Python's relevance in accounting, it's essential to highlight its role in automation. Repetitive tasks that consume a significant amount of time for accountants can be streamlined and automated through Python. Whether it's data entry, report generation, or complex calculations, Python can handle it all.

Benefits of Using Python in Accounting Tasks

Now, let's delve into the benefits of integrating Python into accounting tasks:

1. Enhanced Efficiency: Python is a powerful ally in improving the efficiency of accounting processes. By automating routine tasks, accountants can focus on more critical aspects of their work, such as data analysis, interpretation, and decision-making.

2. Data Manipulation: Python's rich ecosystem of libraries, including Pandas and NumPy, provides accountants with the tools they need to manipulate, clean, and analyze financial data. This is crucial for ensuring the accuracy and reliability of financial reports.

3. Custom Solutions: Python allows accountants to create customized solutions tailored to their specific needs. Whether it's a unique reporting format or a specialized data analysis tool, Python provides the flexibility to develop tailored applications.

4. Error Reduction: Automation with Python significantly reduces the likelihood of errors caused by manual data entry and calculations. This not only saves time but also enhances the accuracy of financial records.

5. Time Savings: Accountants often find themselves bogged down by repetitive tasks. Python's ability to handle these tasks efficiently translates into substantial time savings, which can be

allocated to more strategic activities.

6. Data Visualization: Python's libraries like Matplotlib enable accountants to create visually appealing charts and graphs, making it easier to communicate financial insights to stakeholders.

7. Improved Decision-Making: With Python, accountants can access real-time data, perform complex analyses, and generate reports quickly. This empowers them to make informed decisions that can have a significant impact on the financial health of an organization.

8. Career Advancement: Proficiency in Python is a valuable skill that can set you apart in the job market. Employers seek accountants who can leverage technology to enhance productivity and drive business growth.

Python: The Future of Accounting

It's not an exaggeration to say that Python is shaping the future of accounting. In a world driven by data and analytics, the ability to harness the power of programming languages like Python is becoming increasingly critical. As accounting processes continue to evolve, Python equips professionals with the necessary tools to adapt and thrive in this changing landscape.

This book is your gateway to unlocking the immense potential of Python in the field of accounting. Throughout the chapters that follow, we will guide you through the fundamental concepts, practical applications, and advanced techniques that will empower you to leverage Python to its fullest extent.

As we progress through this book, you will not only learn Python but also understand how to apply it to real-world accounting scenarios. Whether you're a seasoned accountant looking to upskill or a novice eager to explore the possibilities of programming, Python for Accounting is designed to cater to all levels of expertise.

CHAPTER 1: INTRODUCTION TO PYTHON FOR ACCOUNTING

Setting Up Your Python Environment

Welcome to the journey of Python for accounting! In this section, we delve into the practical aspects of getting started with Python in an accounting context. We'll explore the fundamental steps of setting up your Python environment, ensuring you have all the necessary tools at your disposal. Let's dive right in.

When venturing into the world of Python, the first thing you need is the Python interpreter itself. Python is an open-source programming language, and it's highly likely that you already have it installed on your computer. However, it's crucial to ensure that you have the latest version. Python is constantly evolving, with each new release bringing improvements and new features. Having the latest version ensures you have access to the most up-to-date tools and libraries.

If you don't have Python installed, don't worry; we've got you covered. You can download Python from the official website, and the installation process is relatively straightforward. Python is available for various platforms, including Windows, macOS, and Linux. Choose the installer that corresponds to your operating system, run it, and follow the on-screen instructions.

Once Python is up and running, the next essential component is a code editor. While you can write Python code in a plain text editor, using an Integrated Development Environment (IDE) makes the coding process more efficient and enjoyable. IDEs provide a comprehensive environment for coding, debugging, and managing your projects. Here are a few popular choices:

PyCharm: Developed by JetBrains, PyCharm is a powerful Python IDE with a range of features tailored to Python development. It offers code analysis, a visual debugger, and a wide range of plugins.

Visual Studio Code: This free, open-source code editor from Microsoft has gained popularity in the Python community. With Python extensions and a vibrant community, it's a great choice for beginners and experienced developers.

Jupyter Notebook: If you prefer a more interactive and data-focused approach, Jupyter Notebook is an excellent choice. It's widely used for data analysis, visualization, and machine learning.

With your code editor chosen, the next step is to set up a virtual environment. Python virtual environments allow you to create isolated environments for your projects, ensuring that dependencies for one project don't interfere with others. This is especially important when working on multiple accounting projects that may require different packages or library versions.

To create a virtual environment, use the built-in venv module. Open your command line or terminal, navigate to your project directory, and run the following command:

python

python -m venv venv_name

Replace venv_name with the name you want to give to your virtual environment. Once created, you can activate the virtual environment using the appropriate command based on your operating system:

On Windows:

shell

venv_name\Scripts\activate

On macOS and Linux:

shell

source venv_name/bin/activate

Your command prompt should change, indicating that you're now inside the virtual environment. This ensures that any Python packages you install are specific to your project.

Python is known for its extensive library ecosystem, and when it comes to accounting, some libraries stand out. Two essential libraries for accounting tasks are Pandas and NumPy. Pandas provides data structures for efficiently working with structured data, while NumPy is used for numerical operations. We'll explore these libraries in more detail in the subsequent chapters.

To install libraries, you can use the package manager pip, which comes with Python. For instance, to install Pandas, you can simply run:

python

pip install pandas

Now that you have Python installed, an IDE set up, a virtual environment created, and essential libraries installed, you're all set to embark on your Python journey for accounting. This environment provides a clean and organized space for you to start writing Python scripts tailored to your specific accounting needs.

But remember, setting up your environment is just the beginning. In the following chapters, you'll dive into Python's syntax, learn how to work with data, explore advanced libraries, and tackle practical accounting tasks. With the right tools in place, you're well on your way to becoming proficient in Python for accounting.

Feel free to explore Python further, experiment with the libraries, and get comfortable with your chosen IDE. It's all part of the exciting learning process that awaits you. So, let's keep this momentum going as we delve deeper into the world of Python and accounting.

Pythonic Harmony in Syntax:

At its core, Python is celebrated for its readability and simplicity. Pythonic code flows like poetry, and to master it, understanding the syntax is paramount. Every Python program begins with a purpose, and this purpose is expressed through a series of instructions known as statements.

These statements follow a simple rule: one statement per line. Unlike other programming languages, Python doesn't require semicolons or curly braces to define blocks of code. Instead, it relies on indentation, specifically using four spaces to create meaningful code blocks.

Why? To promote clarity and readability. It's like writing a beautiful manuscript where indentation is akin to proper paragraph spacing and punctuation. Let's see it in action:

python

```
if temperature > 30:
    print("It's a hot day!")
else:
    print("Enjoy the weather.")
```

In this example, the indentation is your guide to which code belongs to the 'if' condition and which to the 'else.' This structure forms the essence of Pythonic syntax, making your code not only functional but a pleasure to read and maintain.

The Versatile Variable:

Variables are like containers that store data, and in Python, you don't need to declare the data type explicitly. Python is dynamically typed, which means it figures out the data type on its own. To create a variable, you just choose a name and assign a value to it.

For instance:

python

```
age = 30
name = "Alice"
temperature = 25.5
is_sunny = True
```

In this small code snippet, we've created variables for age (an integer), name (a string), temperature (a float), and is_sunny (a boolean). Python's dynamic typing provides flexibility, allowing you to switch variable types during runtime, making it remarkably versatile.

Data Types Unveiled:

Python offers various built-in data types, each designed to handle different kinds of data. Here are some of the key ones:

Integers (int): Used for whole numbers.

Floating-Point Numbers (float): Used for numbers with a decimal point.

Strings (str): Used for text and characters.

Boolean (bool): Used for True or False values.

Lists and Tuples: Used to store collections of data.

Dictionaries: Used for key-value pairs.

Sets: Used to store unique items.

Consider this Pythonic symphony:

python

```
name = "John"
age = 25
height = 5.11
languages =
person = {"name": name, "age": age, "height": height}
```

Here, we've not only defined variables but also used data structures like lists and dictionaries to store collections of data. The elegant versatility of Python is evident as it effortlessly handles multiple data types with grace and ease.

Expressing with Operators:

Python also provides a rich set of operators to perform operations on variables. You have your basic arithmetic operators like + for addition and - for subtraction, along with others like * for multiplication and / for division.

Then there's the modulo operator %, which helps you find the remainder when dividing one number by another, and the double asterisk ** for exponentiation. These operators are essential for numeric calculations in accounting.

python

```
income = 5000
```

expenses = 3000

profit = income - expenses

tax = profit * 0.2

In this example, we've used these operators to calculate profit and tax based on income and expenses.

Building Blocks of Pythonic Mastery:

Understanding Python's syntax and variables is akin to mastering the fundamentals of any art form. You've learned to structure your code elegantly, define variables, and grasp various data types. Armed with these foundational elements, you're now ready to compose the symphony of Python programs, creating harmonious solutions for accounting tasks.

Data Types: The Pillars of Accounting Analysis

Before delving into the world of variables, it's imperative to have a solid grasp of data types. Data types define the nature of the information you work with, and they play a crucial role in determining how data can be manipulated and processed. In Python, you'll commonly encounter a few data types that are particularly relevant in accounting:

1. Integers (int): These are whole numbers without any decimal points, and they are frequently used in accounting for representing quantities. For example, the number of units in inventory or the count of transactions within a period.

2. Floating-Point Numbers (float): In accounting, you often deal with values that require precision beyond whole numbers. Floating-point numbers include decimals and are suitable for

representing financial amounts. For instance, a company's revenue or expenses.

3. Strings (str): Textual data, such as company names or descriptions of transactions, is stored as strings. These are sequences of characters enclosed in single or double quotation marks.

4. Lists: Lists are versatile data structures to store multiple values. In accounting, you might use lists to hold financial data series over time, like daily stock prices or monthly revenue figures.

5. Dictionaries: Dictionaries allow you to associate values with keys. In accounting, you can use dictionaries to create data structures that map account names to their respective balances.

6. Booleans (bool): Booleans represent either True or False, often used in decision-making processes, such as evaluating financial conditions for investment.

Manipulating Variables: The Art of Accounting

The heart of accounting analysis lies in the ability to manipulate and work with variables effectively. Variables are like containers that hold data, and Python provides a wealth of tools to manage these containers seamlessly. Here's a glimpse of how you can create, modify, and utilize variables:

1. Variable Assignment: In Python, assigning a value to a variable is as simple as using the equal sign. For example, you can assign the integer value 100 to a variable named balance: balance = 100.

2. Variable Types: Variables automatically take on the data type of the value assigned to them. For instance, if you assign the string "Apple" to a variable, it becomes a string variable.

3. Mathematical Operations: Python supports a wide range of mathematical operations, making it easy to perform calculations. For instance, you can calculate the net profit by subtracting expenses from revenue.

python

```
revenue = 5000.50
expenses = 2000.25
net_profit = revenue - expenses
```

4. Concatenation: For strings, you can use the + operator to concatenate them. In accounting, this can be handy for creating custom financial reports with clear headings.

python

```
company_name = "XYZ Corporation"
report_title = "Financial Statement - " + company_name
```

5. Lists and Dictionaries: Lists and dictionaries provide efficient ways to store and manipulate multiple values. Suppose you have daily stock prices. You can store them in a list and perform calculations like finding the average price.

python

HAYDEN VAN DER POST

stock_prices =

average_price = sum(stock_prices) / len(stock_prices)

Dictionaries are useful for organizing financial data, like mapping accounts to their balances.

python

```
financial_data = {
    "Cash": 50000,
    "Accounts Receivable": 25000,
    "Inventory": 100000
}
```

6. Conditional Statements: In accounting, decision-making is crucial. Python's conditional statements like if, else, and elif allow you to make decisions based on the values of variables. For instance, you can check if a company's liquidity ratio is below a certain threshold.

python

```
liquidity_ratio = 1.5
threshold = 1.0

if liquidity_ratio > threshold:
    print("The company has good liquidity.")
else:
    print("The company should improve its liquidity position.")
```

7. Looping: Accounting often involves working with extensive data sets. Python's loops, such as for and while loops, help you iterate through data and perform repetitive tasks efficiently.

In this journey through data types and variables in Python for accounting, you've laid the foundation for understanding and working with financial data. You now possess the tools to represent financial values, organize information, and perform calculations—skills that will prove invaluable in the world of accounting.

Essential Python Libraries for Accounting

As we venture deeper into the world of Python for accounting, it's time to shine a spotlight on the unsung heroes that will power your data analysis and manipulation. These heroes come in the form of Python libraries, and among them, two stand out prominently: Pandas and NumPy. Their role is pivotal in transforming Python into a powerful tool for financial data management and analysis.

Introducing Pandas: Your Data Manipulation Ally

Imagine you're handed a mountain of financial data, possibly in the form of spreadsheets or CSV files, and you need to make sense of it. This is where Pandas comes to the rescue. It's like having a trusted assistant who's an expert at organizing, cleaning, and analyzing data.

Pandas provides data structures and functions that allow you to work with structured data effortlessly. The primary building blocks of Pandas are Series and DataFrames. A Series is like a column in a spreadsheet, while a DataFrame is the whole spreadsheet itself.

Pandas allows you to read data from various file formats, perform data cleaning tasks such as handling missing values and duplicates, and apply filters and transformations. If you need to merge data from different sources or perform complex aggregations, Pandas makes it intuitive.

Let's say you have a CSV file with financial records, and you want to calculate the average income for a specific group of clients. Here's a simple example of how Pandas can help:

python

```python
import pandas as pd

# Read data from a CSV file
data = pd.read_csv('financial_data.csv')

# Filter data for a specific group
selected_data = data == 'ABC Inc']

# Calculate average income
average_income = selected_data.mean()

print(f"The average income for ABC Inc is $
{average_income:.2f}")
```

This example is just a glimpse of what Pandas can do. It's a versatile library that makes managing financial data feel like a breeze.

NumPy: Your Numeric Computing Powerhouse

When it comes to performing mathematical operations and working with numerical data, NumPy is the go-to library. It forms the foundation for Pandas and many other data science libraries, providing support for large, multi-dimensional arrays and matrices, along with a wide variety of high-level mathematical functions.

NumPy simplifies tasks like element-wise operations, mathematical and logical operations on arrays, and random number generation. It's also incredibly efficient, making it suitable for handling large datasets and complex numerical computations.

For instance, let's say you have an array of stock prices and you want to calculate the daily returns. NumPy can help with that:

python

```
import numpy as np

# Define an array of stock prices
stock_prices = np.array()

# Calculate daily returns
daily_returns = (stock_prices - stock_prices) / stock_prices

print("Daily Returns:", daily_returns)
```

With NumPy, you can perform array-wise operations with ease, making it an essential tool for financial modeling and analysis.

The Perfect Synergy

The magic happens when you combine Pandas and NumPy in your financial analysis. Pandas provides the data manipulation and organization capabilities, while NumPy supercharges it with numerical computing power. Together, they create a dynamic duo that can handle a wide range of financial tasks efficiently.

Imagine you have a dataset that includes transaction records and you want to compute the moving average of your account balance. With Pandas, you can easily load and manipulate the data. NumPy, in turn, can be used for the complex moving average calculation, ensuring that your financial analysis is accurate and actionable.

python

```python
import pandas as pd
import numpy as np

# Load transaction data into a Pandas DataFrame
transactions = pd.read_csv('account_transactions.csv')

# Calculate the moving average using NumPy
account_balance = transactions.to_numpy()
moving_average = np.convolve(account_balance, np.ones(30) / 30, mode='valid')

print("Moving Average of Account Balance:", moving_average)
```

In this example, Pandas helps in reading and structuring your data, and NumPy handles the mathematical computation.

Writing Your First Python Script

You might be wondering, what exactly is a Python script? Simply put, a Python script is a set of instructions written in the Python programming language that tells your computer what to do. These instructions can range from basic arithmetic operations to complex data manipulations and much more. Think of Python scripts as the recipe for a delicious dish, where each line of code represents a specific ingredient or cooking step.

Before you dive into writing your first Python script, it's essential to understand the structure of a Python program. In Python, each line of code serves a specific purpose, and the order in which these lines are written matters. Here's a basic structure of a Python script:

python

```
# This is a comment. Comments are for human readers and are
not executed.
# They provide explanations and notes about the code.

# Import necessary libraries or modules
import module_name

# Define variables and assign values to them
variable_name = value
```

```python
# Write functions to perform specific tasks
def function_name(parameters):
    # Function's code here
    return result

# Execute your code
if __name__ == "__main__":
    # Your code here
```

Comments are an essential part of your Python script. They help you and others understand the code's logic and purpose. In Python, comments start with a # symbol, and everything after that symbol on the same line is considered a comment.

Running Your Python Script

Now that you have a basic understanding of Python script structure, it's time to create your first Python program. You can use any text editor to write Python code, and there are specialized Integrated Development Environments (IDEs) designed for Python that offer a more -friendly experience. We covered setting up your Python environment in section 1.2b.

Here's a simple example of a Python script that calculates the sum of two numbers:

python

```python
# This is a comment
# Define two numbers
```

```
num1 = 5
num2 = 7

# Calculate the sum
sum_result = num1 + num2

# Print the result
print("The sum of", num1, "and", num2, "is", sum_result)
```

Save this code in a file with a .py extension, for example, sum.py. You can execute this script from your command line or terminal by navigating to the directory where your script is saved and running the following command:

```
python
```

```
python sum.py
```

Python will execute the code, and you should see the output displayed on your screen: "The sum of 5 and 7 is 12." Congratulations! You've just run your first Python program.

Testing Your Code

Testing is a crucial step in programming. It helps you ensure that your code works as expected and handles different scenarios. As you progress in your Python journey, you'll encounter more complex projects and tasks that demand thorough testing.

Python provides tools and libraries for testing, such as unittest and pytest. These frameworks help you create test cases and run them to verify that your code functions correctly.

Here's a simple example of testing using Python's built-in unittest framework:

python

```
import unittest

def add_numbers(a, b):
    return a + b

class TestAddition(unittest.TestCase):
    def test_add_positive_numbers(self):
        self.assertEqual(add_numbers(3, 5), 8)

    def test_add_negative_numbers(self):
        self.assertEqual(add_numbers(-2, -4), -6)

if __name__ == "__main__":
    unittest.main()
```

In this script, we define a function add_numbers that takes two arguments and returns their sum. We also create a test class TestAddition with two test methods, test_add_positive_numbers and test_add_negative_numbers. These test methods use the assertEqual method to check if the add_numbers function produces the expected results.

When you run this script, the unittest framework will execute the tests and report whether they pass or fail.

This is just the beginning of your Python programming journey. You've learned how to structure a Python script, run it, and even write simple tests. As you continue to explore Python for accounting, you'll delve into more complex applications and gain a deeper understanding of how Python can revolutionize your work in the accounting field.

Debugging and Troubleshooting

On your journey to master Python for accounting, you'll inevitably encounter challenges along the way. This chapter delves into the essential skill of debugging and troubleshooting, a critical aspect of programming. Debugging is not just about finding and fixing errors in your code; it's about developing a systematic approach to problem-solving, enhancing your analytical skills, and ultimately becoming a more proficient Python programmer.

The Nature of Bugs

Let's begin by understanding the nature of bugs in your code. Bugs are those unexpected, frustrating little gremlins that can cause your program to misbehave. They can take various forms, such as syntax errors, logical errors, or even unexpected behavior due to incorrect data handling. Debugging is the process of identifying and rectifying these issues.

Identifying Errors

The first step in debugging is to identify the errors. Python is helpful in this regard because it provides error messages that give you a clue about what went wrong. When you encounter an error, Python typically displays a message that specifies the type of error and the location where it occurred. For example, you might see an error message like:

javascript

SyntaxError: invalid syntax

This tells you that there's a problem with the syntax of your code. It's important to carefully read these messages, as they often contain valuable hints about what needs to be fixed.

Systematic Debugging Approach

To effectively debug your code, it's essential to follow a systematic approach. Here's a step-by-step guide to debugging:

Reproduce the Error: First, try to reproduce the error consistently. Understanding the conditions that trigger the bug is crucial.

Check the Error Message: Pay close attention to the error message. It typically includes a line number where the error occurred. This is your starting point.

Inspect the Code: Go to the line indicated by the error message and review the code around it. Look for any obvious issues like typos, missing parentheses, or incorrect variable names.

Use Print Statements: Sometimes, inserting print statements in your code can help you trace the flow and values of variables. This is a simple but effective way to pinpoint where things go wrong.

Divide and Conquer: If the error remains elusive, try dividing your code into smaller parts and testing them individually. This can help you isolate the problematic section.

Leverage Debugging Tools: Python provides debugging tools like pdb, which allows you to set breakpoints, inspect variables, and step through your code line by line. Learning to use these tools can be a game-changer.

Documentation and Comments: Ensure that your code is well-documented. Sometimes, the act of explaining your code in comments can help you spot errors.

Seek Help: Don't hesitate to seek help from the Python community or colleagues. Often, a fresh pair of eyes can quickly identify what you might have missed.

Common Debugging Strategies

Beyond the systematic approach, there are some common debugging strategies that can help you troubleshoot effectively:

Syntax Errors: For syntax errors, Python is usually explicit about what's wrong. Ensure that your code adheres to Python's syntax rules.

Print Statements: Insert print statements to display variable values at different points in your code. This can reveal unexpected values or the flow of your program.

Unit Testing: Create unit tests for your code. These are small, focused tests that verify specific parts of your code. When a test fails, it pinpoints the issue.

Online Resources: Take advantage of online resources and forums. Websites like Stack Overflow are excellent places to find solutions to common problems.

Code Review: If you're working in a team, consider having your code reviewed by a colleague. Fresh perspectives can uncover issues you might have overlooked.

Now, let's put this knowledge into practice with a simple Python code example:

python

```python
# Debugging Example
def divide_numbers(a, b):
    result = a / b
    return result

# Calling the function with a potential issue
result = divide_numbers(10, 0)
print(result)
```

In this code, we have a division by zero, which is a common runtime error. When you run this code, Python will raise a ZeroDivisionError. It's important to understand the error message, locate the issue, and handle it correctly.

Understanding how to tackle bugs in your Python code is a crucial skill for any programmer, and as you progress in your Python journey, you'll find that debugging becomes second nature.

Conclusion

Chapter 1 Has Been A Foundational Journey Into The World Of
Python And Its Relevance In Accounting. You've Explored The
Fundamental Aspects Of Python Programming, From Setting
Up Your Development Environment To Understanding Basic
Syntax And Data Types. We've Also Introduced You To Essential
Python Libraries For Accounting And Guided You Through
Writing Your First Python Program. You've Gained Insights
Into Debugging And Troubleshooting—Vital Skills For Any
Programmer.

As you reflect on your progress, remember that Python for
accounting is not just about learning a programming language;
it's about transforming your ability to work with financial
data efficiently and creatively. In Chapter 2, "Data Handling
and Visualization," we'll take a deeper dive into the practical
application of Python in accounting. You'll learn how to work
with financial data, clean and transform it, and visualize the
results to derive valuable insights. This hands-on experience
will empower you to harness the true potential of Python in the
field of accounting. So, let's embark on this next chapter, where
you'll uncover the power of data-driven decision-making.

CHAPTER 2: DATA HANDLING AND VISUALIZATION

Welcome to Chapter 2 of "Python for Accounting." In this chapter, we delve into the intriguing world of data handling and visualization, showcasing how Python can revolutionize the way accountants work with financial data. This chapter is all about taking raw financial data and transforming it into valuable insights that drive informed decision-making.

We will explore the critical processes of working with CSV files, cleaning and transforming data, and visualizing financial information with the help of Python. Each section in this chapter equips you with the skills and knowledge to navigate the vast sea of financial data, making it more manageable, insightful, and actionable.

Working with CSV Files

In the ever-evolving landscape of accounting, one thing remains constant—data. Financial data is the lifeblood of any accounting practice, and mastering the art of handling and visualizing it can make all the difference. In this chapter, we're going to unravel the magic of working with CSV files and using Python to transform raw data into actionable insights. So, fasten your seatbelts and get ready to embark on this data-driven journey.

Our discussion begins with one of the most common formats for storing tabular data—CSV files. Comma-Separated Values (CSV) files are simple, yet incredibly powerful, because they can store data in a structured way that is easy for both humans and machines to read. If you've ever worked with Excel spreadsheets, you're already familiar with the concept.

But here's the kicker: Python, with its extensive libraries, makes handling CSV files a breeze. With just a few lines of code, you can read, manipulate, and write data to and from CSV files. This flexibility opens up a world of possibilities for accountants.

Reading CSV Files

Imagine having a vast dataset of financial transactions in a CSV file. Python allows you to swiftly read this data into your scripts, providing a foundation for various accounting tasks. Let's take a look at a simple example:

python

```python
import csv

# Open the CSV file
with open('financial_data.csv', mode='r') as file:
    # Create a CSV reader
    csv_reader = csv.reader(file)

    # Iterate through rows
    for row in csv_reader:
```

```
      print(row)
```

In this code snippet, we import Python's built-in csv module and use it to read a CSV file named financial_data.csv. This code reads each row of the CSV and prints it to the console.

Writing to CSV Files

It's not just about reading data; you can also use Python to write data back to CSV files, which is crucial for saving the results of your analyses or generating reports. Here's a simple example:

python

```
import csv

data = ,
    ,
    ,
    # Add more rows as needed
]

with open('accounting_ledger.csv', mode='w', newline='') as file:
    csv_writer = csv.writer(file)

    for row in data:
        csv_writer.writerow(row)
```

In this snippet, we create a list called data, where each element is a list representing a row of the CSV. We then use the csv module to write this data to a new CSV file, 'accounting_ledger.csv'. This is just the tip of the iceberg when it comes to working with CSV files, and you'll explore more advanced techniques as you progress through this chapter.

Importing Financial Data for Analysis

As an accountant, you're well aware of the importance of clean and well-structured data. CSV files are a common format for exchanging financial data, and being proficient in importing them can save you time and reduce errors. Whether it's importing transaction records, expense reports, or income statements, Python's versatility will empower you to streamline your workflow and maintain data integrity.

But handling CSV files is just the beginning of our journey in data handling and visualization. In the following sections, we'll dive deeper into data cleaning and transformation, data visualization using Matplotlib, exploratory data analysis (EDA), and specialized techniques for visualizing financial data.

By mastering the art of working with CSV files in Python, you've taken your first steps into the world of data handling. You've learned how to read and write data from and to CSV files, a skill that will prove invaluable in your accounting endeavors. In the next section, we'll venture into the realm of data cleaning and transformation, where we'll explore techniques to ensure the data you work with is pristine and ready for analysis. So, buckle up for an exciting ride into the world of data refinement and preparation.

Cleaning the Raw Data: A Prerequisite for Analysis

Before you can embark on any data analysis task, you must ensure that the data you're working with is of high quality. Raw data can be messy and riddled with imperfections, which can skew your analysis and lead to erroneous conclusions. This is where data cleaning comes into play.

Data cleaning involves identifying and addressing various data anomalies, such as missing values, duplicate records, and inconsistent formatting. Python offers a variety of tools and libraries to assist in this process, making it a powerful ally in your quest for pristine data.

Handling Missing Values: Filling in the Blanks

One common issue you'll encounter when dealing with real-world data is missing values. Missing data can disrupt your analysis, and a thoughtful strategy is needed to address this challenge. Python provides multiple techniques to manage missing values, from simple imputation to more advanced methods.

For instance, you can use Python's Pandas library to replace missing values with the mean or median of the column, eliminating gaps while preserving data integrity. Alternatively, advanced methods, such as predictive modeling, can be employed to infer missing values based on the patterns observed in the available data. These techniques not only fill in the blanks but also contribute to more robust analyses.

Addressing Outliers: Separating the Signal from the Noise

Outliers, or data points significantly different from the majority, can distort your analysis results. They might be errors or valid data points with unique characteristics. Handling outliers effectively is vital in ensuring the reliability of your analysis.

Python equips you with a range of statistical techniques to detect and address outliers. You can visualize data distributions using libraries like Matplotlib and Seaborn to identify potential outliers. Additionally, you can use Z-scores or the Interquartile Range (IQR) to detect and manage these extreme values.

Data Transformation: Reshaping for Analysis

Once your data is cleaned and free of anomalies, it's time to think about transforming it to meet the specific requirements of your analysis. Transformation can involve converting data types, aggregating data, or creating new features that provide deeper insights.

Python's Pandas library is a versatile tool for data transformation. It allows you to reshape your data, apply functions to columns, and even merge datasets when dealing with data from multiple sources. Moreover, you can manipulate data to generate calculated columns, which are often essential in financial analysis.

Putting Theory into Practice: Python Code Examples

To illustrate the concepts of data cleaning and transformation, let's dive into Python code examples. Imagine you have a dataset containing monthly sales data for a retail company. It's your task to clean and transform this data for analysis.

First, we'll address missing values by filling them with the mean value of the respective column:

python

```python
import pandas as pd

# Load the dataset
data = pd.read_csv('sales_data.csv')

# Fill missing values with the mean
data.fillna(data.mean(), inplace=True)
```

Next, we'll detect and manage outliers using the IQR method:

python

```python
Q1 = data.quantile(0.25)
Q3 = data.quantile(0.75)
IQR = Q3 - Q1

# Define upper and lower bounds
lower_bound = Q1 - 1.5 * IQR
upper_bound = Q3 + 1.5 * IQR

# Remove outliers
data = data >= lower_bound) & (data <= upper_bound)]
```

Finally, we'll transform the data by calculating the monthly revenue and adding it as a new column:

python

```python
data = data * data
```

These examples showcase how Python, with its powerful libraries, can be your trusty companion in the quest for clean, well-prepared data.

Data cleaning and transformation are crucial steps in the data analysis process. With Python as your tool of choice, you can efficiently manage missing values, address outliers, and reshape data to unlock the true potential of your datasets. Armed with these skills, you'll be better prepared to navigate the complex landscape of financial analysis and accounting, leveraging data as a valuable resource for informed decision-making.

Data Visualization with Matplotlib

In the world of Python for accounting, data visualization plays a pivotal role. It's not just about collecting and crunching numbers; it's also about presenting your findings in a way that makes sense to others. Matplotlib, one of the most versatile and widely-used data visualization libraries, empowers accountants with the tools they need to create impactful charts and graphs.

The Art of Visualization

Picture this: you've gathered a substantial amount of financial data, diligently processed it, and now it's time to share your insights with the stakeholders. You could present them with raw numbers and spreadsheets, but there's a more effective way to convey your findings. Visualizations, when done right, can reveal patterns, outliers, and trends that might otherwise go unnoticed.

Why Matplotlib?

Matplotlib is a Python library that has become the gold standard for creating static, animated, and interactive visualizations in Python. While Python offers a range of data visualization libraries, Matplotlib is often the go-to choice because of its flexibility and customizability. It provides a solid foundation for creating various types of plots, including bar charts, line charts, scatter plots, and more.

Getting Started

To embark on your journey with Matplotlib, you first need to ensure you have it installed. Most Python distributions include Matplotlib by default, but if it's not already installed, you can easily do so using pip:

python

pip install matplotlib

Once you have Matplotlib ready, the possibilities are almost endless. Let's consider a scenario in which you've been tasked with visualizing quarterly revenue trends for your organization.

Plotting with Matplotlib

Suppose you've collected quarterly revenue data for the past five years and want to create a line chart that showcases the trends. Here's a step-by-step guide on how to do it:

python

Import the Matplotlib library

```python
import matplotlib.pyplot as plt

# Data for your line chart
quarters =
years =
revenue = ,

    ,

    ,

    ,

]

# Create a line chart
for i, year in enumerate(years):
    plt.plot(quarters, revenue, label=year)

# Add labels and a legend
plt.xlabel('Quarters')
plt.ylabel('Revenue (in USD)')
plt.title('Quarterly Revenue Trends (2018-2022)')
plt.legend()

# Display the chart
plt.show()
```

In this example, we import Matplotlib, define our data, create a line chart, add labels for the x and y-axes, set a title, and display the chart. The result is a clear and visually appealing representation of the revenue trends over five years.

Customization and Beyond

Matplotlib offers extensive customization options. You can change colors, styles, markers, and more to make your visualizations uniquely tailored to your needs. This flexibility enables you to create professional and insightful reports for your clients and colleagues.

While this example focuses on a line chart, Matplotlib can be used to generate a wide range of visualizations, including bar charts, histograms, pie charts, and heatmaps. The library is also suitable for creating visual summaries of large datasets, exploring distributions, and identifying correlations.

Whether you're presenting budget allocations, expense breakdowns, or investment portfolios, Matplotlib allows you to craft visuals that enhance your storytelling and facilitate better decision-making.

A Path to Mastery

As with any skill, mastering data visualization with Matplotlib takes practice. The key is not only to create visually appealing charts but also to ensure they effectively convey your message. Experiment, explore, and dive deep into the Matplotlib documentation to unlock its full potential.

Exploratory Data Analysis (EDA)

Exploratory Data Analysis, often abbreviated as EDA, is a critical phase in the world of data analysis. In this chapter, we delve into the world of EDA, a process that bridges the gap between the raw data you've acquired and the valuable insights you're striving to extract. Just like an archaeologist examining ancient artifacts, you, as an accountant armed with Python, will unearth meaningful patterns and anomalies hidden in the data.

So, why is EDA important? To answer this question, let's step into the shoes of an accountant who's just received a massive dataset filled with financial records. The numbers and figures may seem like an impenetrable fortress at first glance. This is where EDA comes to your rescue.

The Art of Exploration

EDA is a systematic approach to making sense of your data. It's like a treasure hunt where you're searching for the gems of knowledge hidden within the numbers. It involves summarizing the main characteristics of your data, often with the help of graphical representations, to understand its structure and identify patterns.

The first step in EDA is always to get acquainted with your data. Think of it as an introduction to a new acquaintance. You wouldn't dive right into business; you'd start with some small talk. Similarly, in EDA, you begin by understanding the basic attributes of your data. What does it look like? What are its key features?

One essential technique at this stage is data summarization, which helps you to get a snapshot of your data's characteristics. In Python, libraries like Pandas are your trusted companions. You can use functions like describe() to get descriptive statistics, revealing information about the central tendency, dispersion, and shape of the dataset.

Data Visualization: The Artist's Brush

Once you've got a grasp of your data's essence, it's time to transform it into visual artwork. Imagine you're a painter, and the canvas is your data. This is where data visualization comes into play. One of the most potent tools at your disposal is Matplotlib.

Matplotlib is like a painter's palette, offering you a variety of options to choose from, allowing you to paint a vivid picture of your data. You can create stunning charts, graphs, and plots to represent your data visually. These visual representations help you spot trends, anomalies, and outliers more effectively than scanning through endless rows and columns.

For instance, when dealing with financial data, you may want to visualize stock prices over time, detect seasonality, or identify any sudden spikes or dips. Matplotlib empowers you to craft line plots, bar charts, and candlestick charts that breathe life into your data, making it easier to spot patterns that may have been hidden in plain sight.

Detecting Trends and Anomalies

Identifying trends and anomalies is where the detective work begins. EDA provides you with the magnifying glass to scrutinize the data closely. You want to see where the data is leading you, and whether it is in line with what you expect.

Common techniques used in this stage include:

Time Series Analysis: If your data involves a time component, this is your go-to tool. You'll learn how to analyze data over time, identify cyclical patterns, and make predictions using Python.

Correlation Analysis: You'll explore relationships between variables. For example, you might examine whether there's a correlation between a company's revenue and its expenses. Python, with libraries like NumPy, makes the computation of correlation coefficients a breeze.

Outlier Detection: Outliers can significantly impact your analysis. Python equips you with the tools to identify and deal with these anomalies, ensuring that they don't distort your insights.

Distribution Analysis: Understanding the distribution of data is vital. Python offers various statistical tests and visualization techniques to reveal the distribution of your data, whether it follows a normal distribution or takes on some other form.

The Power of Python Code

Now, as promised, let's dive into a Python code example to illustrate some of these concepts. Imagine you have a dataset of daily stock prices, and you want to identify any significant fluctuations in the stock prices over time. You'll utilize Matplotlib to create a line plot, making it easier to spot trends or anomalies.

python

```python
import matplotlib.pyplot as plt
import pandas as pd

# Load your financial data into a DataFrame
```

```
df = pd.read_csv("stock_prices.csv")

# Extract date and stock price columns
date = df
price = df

# Create a line plot to visualize the stock prices over time
plt.figure(figsize=(12, 6))
plt.plot(date, price, marker='o', linestyle='-')
plt.title("Stock Prices Over Time")
plt.xlabel("Date")
plt.ylabel("Stock Price")
plt.grid(True)
plt.xticks(rotation=45)
plt.show()
```

This Python code demonstrates the power of data visualization using Matplotlib. It loads financial data from a CSV file, extracts the date and stock price columns, and then plots the stock prices over time. The resulting line plot provides a clear visual representation of the stock price trends.

Exploratory Data Analysis is an art, a science, and a detective's toolkit all in one. With Python and Matplotlib as your partners, you can unlock the hidden stories within your financial data. So, don your detective's hat and embark on the adventure of understanding the intricate world of financial numbers through the lens of EDA.

Financial Data Visualization

In accounting, the ability to visualize financial data is akin to possessing a map through a complex terrain. In this chapter, we delve into specialized techniques for financial data visualization, equipping you with the skills to create informative financial plots that will not only make your analysis more insightful but also enhance your ability to communicate findings effectively.

The Art of Visualizing Financial Data

Before we embark on discovering the intricacies of financial data visualization, it's crucial to recognize the fundamental significance of this skill. Visualizations serve as the bridge between raw numbers and comprehensible insights. They can bring data to life, revealing trends, patterns, and anomalies that might otherwise remain hidden in spreadsheets.

In the world of accounting, where precision and clarity are paramount, effective data visualization can transform a mound of numbers into a compelling narrative. Whether you're presenting financial reports to stakeholders, conducting internal audits, or analyzing market trends, the power of visualization cannot be overstated.

Selecting the Right Visualization Techniques

One of the first steps in mastering financial data visualization is understanding that not all charts and graphs are created equal. Different scenarios call for distinct visualization techniques. Let's explore some of the most relevant ones:

Line Charts: These are your go-to for showing trends over time. Whether you're tracking revenue growth or assessing market fluctuations, line charts reveal the direction and magnitude of change.

Bar Charts: Perfect for comparing categories. If you're analyzing expenses across different departments or evaluating the performance of multiple investments, bar charts provide clear comparisons.

Pie Charts: While somewhat controversial, they can effectively show the composition of a whole. Use pie charts when you want to display the proportion of various expenses in a budget, for instance.

Scatter Plots: Ideal for identifying relationships between variables. In accounting, you might use scatter plots to explore correlations between factors like advertising spending and sales revenue.

Heatmaps: These are excellent for presenting multidimensional data. For instance, you can use a heatmap to illustrate spending patterns across different quarters or departments.

Candlestick Charts: Widely employed in finance for visualizing stock prices, candlestick charts reveal price movements and provide insights into market sentiment.

The Role of Data Storytelling

Once you've chosen the right visualization technique for your data, the next step is to weave a narrative around it. Your visualizations should not stand alone; they should be part of a coherent story that guides the viewer through the data.

Begin by defining the context of your visualization. What question or issue does it address? For example, are you visualizing the allocation of a marketing budget to assess its effectiveness?

Then, introduce your visualization with a concise but informative caption. This caption should provide context and draw the viewer's attention to the key takeaway. Avoid vague titles like "Chart 1" and opt for descriptive ones like "Quarterly Marketing Spend Distribution."

As you present your financial data using charts and graphs, remember to annotate and label. Add axis labels, data points, and any relevant annotations that help clarify the message. For example, if you're presenting a line chart of revenue growth, annotate the points where significant changes occurred.

Let's take a look at a simple example of using Matplotlib to create a line chart depicting quarterly revenue growth:

python

```
import matplotlib.pyplot as plt

# Sample data
quarters =
revenue =

# Create a line chart
plt.plot(quarters, revenue, marker='o', linestyle='-')
```

```
# Adding labels and title
plt.xlabel("Quarters")
plt.ylabel("Revenue (in USD)")
plt.title("Quarterly Revenue Growth")

# Display the chart
plt.show()
```

This code snippet generates a line chart showing quarterly revenue. You can customize the appearance of the chart, add labels and titles, and ultimately create a visualization that tells a compelling story about your financial data.

Financial data visualization is an indispensable skill for accountants. It transforms raw data into actionable insights and facilitates effective communication. Remember, selecting the right visualization technique, storytelling, and leveraging Python's libraries like Matplotlib and Seaborn will empower you to convey your financial findings with clarity and impact.

The Canvas of Customization

Your canvas is the digital screen, and your palette consists of various parameters and attributes. Customization is the brush that paints life into your visualizations. But why is it so crucial?

Enhanced Communication: Customization allows you to emphasize specific data points or trends, making your message clearer and more compelling.

Branding: For those creating visualizations for businesses

or organizations, customization ensures that your charts and graphs align with the brand's visual identity.

Engagement: Well-designed and visually appealing charts capture your audience's attention and keep them engaged, even with complex data.

Clarity: By adding labels, titles, and other custom elements, you enhance the clarity of your visualizations, guiding your audience's understanding.

The Palette of Customization

Colors:

Selecting an appropriate color scheme can drastically affect the readability and aesthetics of your charts. Use contrasting colors for different data elements to ensure they stand out. Remember, colorblind-friendly palettes are essential for broader accessibility.

Labels and Titles:

Every element in your chart should be labeled correctly. Use descriptive and concise labels for axes, data points, and legends. Titles should provide context and capture the essence of the visualization.

Custom Styles:

Styles go beyond colors. They encompass line types, marker styles, and font choices. Customizing these aspects allows you to match the visualization with your overall presentation or branding.

Annotations:

Annotations are a powerful way to draw attention to specific data points or trends. You can add text annotations, arrows, or shapes to highlight key findings.

Legends:

Legends are crucial when dealing with multiple data series. Customize legends to make them informative yet unobtrusive. You can change their position, orientation, or style to fit your design.

The Brush Strokes of Customization

Now, let's explore how to implement these customizations in Python. We'll use the Matplotlib library, one of the most popular tools for data visualization.

```python
import matplotlib.pyplot as plt
import numpy as np

# Sample data
x = np.linspace(0, 2 * np.pi, 100)
y = np.sin(x)

# Creating the figure and axis
fig, ax = plt.subplots()

# Customizing the line
ax.plot(x, y, label='Sine Wave', color='blue', linestyle='--', marker='o', markersize=4, markerfacecolor='red',
```

```
markeredgecolor='red')

# Customizing axes labels and title
ax.set_xlabel('Time')
ax.set_ylabel('Amplitude')
ax.set_title('Customized Sine Wave')

# Adding annotations
ax.annotate('Local Maximum', xy=(1.5, 1), xytext=(3, 1.5),
arrowprops=dict(facecolor='black', shrink=0.05))
ax.annotate('Local Minimum', xy=(4.7, -1), xytext=(3, -1.5),
arrowprops=dict(facecolor='black', shrink=0.05))

# Customizing the legend
ax.legend(loc='upper right', fontsize=8)

# Displaying the plot
plt.show()
```

In this example, we customize the sine wave plot with various elements. We set the line color, style, markers, labels, title, and even add annotations. The result is a customized plot that effectively communicates the data.

Mastering the Art

Customization is not just about making your visualizations visually appealing; it's about enhancing their communicative power. By thoughtfully applying color, labels, styles, and other elements, you can transform your data into compelling narratives that resonate with your audience.

Customizing Plots and Graphs

Customization is often the key to conveying your message effectively. Raw data, no matter how insightful, can be challenging to digest without the right presentation. In this section, we're going to delve into the art of tailoring your visualizations, ensuring that your data speaks with clarity and precision.

The Power of Customization

Visualizations are your canvas, and customization is your brush. When working with financial data, you'll often find that standard plots and graphs don't quite cut it. A standard plot might show your data, but a customized plot can tell your data's story.

By customizing your visualizations, you can enhance their communicative power and make them uniquely suited to your audience. Let's explore some ways to achieve this:

Adding Labels

Every plot or graph tells a story, and every story needs a title. Whether you're creating a bar chart, a scatter plot, or a line graph, make sure to provide a clear and concise title that encapsulates what your visualization represents.

For instance, if you're plotting the quarterly revenue of a company, your title could be something like "Company XYZ Quarterly Revenue (2023)." This title immediately conveys the essential information to your audience.

Labelling Axes

Axes on a graph provide context and scale to the data. They tell the viewer what is being measured and in what units. It's essential to label both the x-axis (usually the horizontal one) and the y-axis (typically the vertical one) to prevent any confusion.

In our revenue example, you might label the x-axis "Quarter" and the y-axis "Revenue in USD ($)." Clear and consistent labeling is crucial for your audience to understand the significance of the data points.

Adding Custom Styles

Custom styles go beyond just colors; they encompass everything from line types to marker shapes. When dealing with financial data, you might want to distinguish between different financial instruments or time periods. Custom styles allow you to do this effectively.

For instance, you could represent one financial instrument with a solid line and another with a dashed line. Additionally, you might use circles as markers for data points from one year and squares for another. This level of detail aids your audience in differentiating between data series or categories.

Annotating Data Points

Sometimes, you want to highlight specific data points, such as significant events or outliers. Annotations provide a way to add textual or graphical cues to your visualization. This not only enhances the understanding but also adds depth to your story.

For example, you could use annotations to mark the point at which a company achieved record-breaking revenue. This offers readers a clear visual indication of a pivotal moment.

Providing Legends

Legends are crucial when you're dealing with multiple data series or categories. Without a legend, your audience might struggle to understand which line, bar, or point corresponds to which dataset.

In our financial data example, if you're plotting the revenues of multiple companies on the same graph, a legend can differentiate between them. Each company's name paired with a unique color or symbol ensures clarity.

Python in Action

To grasp the concept better, let's dive into some Python code. We'll be using the Matplotlib library, one of the most popular libraries for data visualization in Python.

python

```python
import matplotlib.pyplot as plt

# Sample data
quarters =
company_a_revenue =
company_b_revenue =

# Creating the plot
plt.plot(quarters, company_a_revenue, label='Company A', color='b', marker='o', linestyle='-', linewidth=2)
```

```
plt.plot(quarters, company_b_revenue, label='Company B',
color='g', marker='s', linestyle='--', linewidth=2)

# Adding labels and title
plt.xlabel('Quarter')
plt.ylabel('Revenue in USD ($)')
plt.title('Company Revenue Comparison (2023)')

# Adding a legend
plt.legend()

# Adding annotations
plt.annotate('Record Break', xy=(quarters, company_a_revenue),
xytext=(3.5, 310000), arrowprops=dict(facecolor='black',
shrink=0.05))

# Displaying the plot
plt.show()
```

In this Python code, we create a line plot comparing the revenues of two companies over four quarters. We've customized the plot by specifying colors, markers, line styles, and annotations, making the visualization more informative and engaging.

Customization is an art that requires practice, but it's well worth the effort. Your Python code can be your artistic tool, and Matplotlib offers a wide range of customization options to bring your data to life.

So, when presenting your financial insights through Python, remember that the power to tell a compelling story lies in the details. Tailoring your visualizations is the key to guiding your audience through the intricate world of accounting data. With practice and a creative touch, you'll master the art of data storytelling.

Data Handling and Visualization

In the previous sections of this book, you've gained a solid foundation in Python for accounting, delving into various aspects of data handling, cleaning, transformation, visualization, and financial analysis. Now, it's time to put your knowledge to the test through practical exercises and a comprehensive case study.

The journey of mastering Python for accounting is not just about understanding the theory; it's about applying what you've learned to real-world scenarios. This hands-on experience will deepen your understanding and prepare you for the challenges accountants face in today's data-driven world.

Case Study: Applying Your Skills

Now, it's time for the main event—the case study. In this comprehensive case study, you'll be dealing with a complex financial scenario that requires you to utilize all the skills you've acquired throughout the book.

Imagine you're working for a medium-sized company that has recently expanded its operations. As the in-house accountant, you're tasked with analyzing the financial data of the various divisions to provide insights into their performance. Your findings will be crucial for the company's future strategic decisions.

In this case study, you'll be required to:

Data Collection and Cleaning: Retrieve data from different sources and ensure it's clean and accurate, just as you learned in Section 2.1 and 2.2.

Data Visualization: Create visualizations to represent financial performance over time and make it easier for stakeholders to grasp the information (Section 2.3 and 2.4).

Financial Analysis: Calculate various financial ratios, assess the risk, and provide forecasts for different divisions (Section 3.1 to 3.4).

Performance Metrics: Develop dashboards that effectively communicate the financial health of each division (Section 3.6).

Automated Reporting: As an extra challenge, create Python scripts to automate the generation of reports, as you've learned in Section 4.3.

The case study will not only test your skills but also provide you with a real sense of achievement as you work through the intricacies of a practical financial analysis.

By the end of the case study, you'll not only have a well-rounded understanding of Python's applications in accounting but also a portfolio-worthy project to showcase your abilities to potential employers or clients.

Throughout this journey, remember that learning Python for accounting is a continuous process. Each challenge you face and overcome will make you a more proficient accountant and a more skilled Python practitioner.

In the upcoming chapters, we'll explore more advanced topics and applications, such as machine learning, natural language processing, and blockchain in accounting. These skills will further broaden your horizons, allowing you to stay at the forefront of technology in the accounting industry.

For now, embrace the practice exercises and the case study as an opportunity to sharpen your skills, and soon you'll find yourself confidently mastering Python for accounting.

Python Code Example: In this section, we'll provide a sample Python code snippet that demonstrates how to create an informative financial chart using Matplotlib. This code will help you get started with the practice exercises and the case study.

python

```python
import matplotlib.pyplot as plt

# Sample financial data
years =
revenue =

# Creating a line chart
plt.plot(years, revenue, marker='o', linestyle='-')

# Adding labels and title
plt.xlabel('Years')
plt.ylabel('Revenue (in USD)')
```

```
plt.title('Company Revenue Over Time')

# Display the chart
plt.show()
```

This simple example showcases how Python can be used to create clear and informative financial visualizations, an essential skill in accounting and financial analysis. As you progress through the practice exercises and the case study, you'll build on this foundation, creating more sophisticated and valuable charts.

Conclusion

In conclusion, Chapter 2 has equipped you with essential skills for data handling and visualization in the realm of Python for accounting. You've learned to navigate and clean financial data, create meaningful visualizations, and set the stage for deeper financial analysis.

As we move forward to Chapter 3, we'll delve into the world of financial analysis with Python. Get ready to explore the intricate world of financial statements, ratios, time series analysis, and forecasting. We'll uncover how Python can be your ally in deciphering financial complexities and guiding informed decision-making. Join us on this analytical journey, and let's unlock the true power of Python in accounting.

CHAPTER 3: FINANCIAL ANALYSIS WITH PYTHON

Welcome to Chapter 3: Financial Analysis with Python. In this chapter, we transition into the heart of Python's role in accounting – financial analysis. You've already built a strong foundation in Python basics, data handling, and visualization. Now, it's time to put your skills to work as we explore the art of deciphering financial data.

This chapter takes you on a journey through the fascinating world of financial statements, ratios, time series analysis, forecasting, risk assessment, and performance metrics. You'll discover how Python empowers accountants to make sound financial decisions, predict future trends, and evaluate the health of an organization's financial performance.

With the knowledge gained in this chapter, you'll be equipped to conduct comprehensive financial analyses, optimize budgeting, and implement strategic risk management. Join us as we embark on this analytical adventure, harnessing the power of Python to navigate the intricate landscape of accounting.

Introduction to Financial Statements

Financial statements are the lifeblood of accounting. They are the vital records that encapsulate a company's financial health and provide a snapshot of its financial performance over a specific period. In this section, we delve into the core of financial analysis, focusing on the essence and significance of financial statements, while equipping you with the Python tools necessary to extract, prepare, and analyze these statements effectively.

The Essence of Financial Statements

Financial statements consist of three key reports: the income statement, the balance sheet, and the cash flow statement. These documents provide essential insights into the financial state of an organization and are fundamental in decision-making processes. Let's briefly explore each one:

Income Statement: Also known as the profit and loss statement, the income statement shows a company's revenues and expenses over a specific period. By analyzing this statement, you can determine whether a business is profitable and how well it is operating.

Balance Sheet: The balance sheet provides a summary of a company's assets, liabilities, and shareholders' equity at a particular point in time. It gives you an understanding of a company's financial position.

Cash Flow Statement: This statement details how changes in the balance sheet and income statements affect cash and cash equivalents. It's crucial for assessing an organization's liquidity and solvency.

Preparing Financial Data for Analysis

Before you can dive into financial analysis, you must first gather and prepare financial data. This involves extracting information from various sources, organizing it, and formatting it for analysis. Python, with its powerful libraries like Pandas, is your key to handling this crucial step efficiently.

Let's look at how Python can assist in the preparation of financial data:

Data Extraction: Python can access data from various sources, such as databases, spreadsheets, or online platforms. Whether you're fetching data from an accounting system or external financial databases, Python streamlines the process.

Data Transformation: Financial data often requires cleaning and transformation. This may involve handling missing values, dealing with different currencies, or aggregating data from various departments. Python can automate these tasks, ensuring data accuracy and consistency.

Data Integration: In a real-world accounting scenario, data often comes from multiple sources. Python can help integrate and consolidate this data into a single dataset, making it ready for analysis.

By utilizing Python's data manipulation capabilities, you save valuable time and minimize errors in preparing financial data, setting the stage for accurate and efficient financial analysis.

The Power of Python in Financial Analysis

Now, why should you use Python for financial analysis? Python, being a versatile and widely adopted programming language, offers several key advantages:

Automation: Python allows you to automate repetitive financial analysis tasks, saving you time and reducing the risk of errors. This automation is crucial when dealing with large datasets.

Customization: Python provides the flexibility to create customized financial analysis models tailored to the specific needs of your organization or clients. You're not limited to prepackaged software.

Scalability: Python can handle both small- and large-scale financial analysis projects. Whether you're working with a startup or a multinational corporation, Python's capabilities scale with your needs.

Community and Libraries: The Python community is vast and active, resulting in a wealth of libraries and resources for financial analysis. Libraries like NumPy and Pandas are invaluable for data manipulation and analysis.

In this chapter, you'll discover how to utilize Python to extract financial data, understand financial statements, and lay the groundwork for financial analysis. We'll explore the practical applications and benefits of Python for interpreting the income statement, balance sheet, and cash flow statement, enabling you to make informed decisions and drive financial strategies with confidence.

Are you ready to unlock the potential of financial statements with Python? Let's embark on this journey to transform raw financial data into meaningful insights, starting with a deep dive into the structure and importance of financial statements.

Calculating Financial Ratios

Financial analysis is the bedrock of accounting, and in this chapter, we delve into the world of financial ratios. These ratios are the vital signs of any organization, providing a window into its financial health. You'll come to understand the mechanics of these ratios and how Python empowers accountants to perform in-depth financial analysis with ease.

Financial ratios are like pieces of a puzzle, each revealing a different aspect of a company's performance. As an accountant, your role is to assemble these pieces to create a comprehensive picture that helps stakeholders make informed decisions. In this section, we'll explore various financial ratios, from liquidity and profitability to solvency and efficiency ratios. You'll learn how to extract the necessary financial data, calculate these ratios, and interpret the results using Python.

Liquidity Ratios

One of the first things you'll discover in the world of financial ratios are liquidity ratios. These ratios assess a company's short-term financial health by measuring its ability to meet its current obligations. Common liquidity ratios include the current ratio, quick ratio, and working capital ratio. Python enables you to automate the retrieval of financial data and compute these ratios efficiently.

For example, to calculate the current ratio:

python

```python
current_assets = 1000000 # Replace with actual values
current_liabilities = 500000
current_ratio = current_assets / current_liabilities
```

Profitability Ratios

Profitability ratios provide insight into a company's ability to generate earnings in relation to its expenses and other costs. Key profitability ratios include gross profit margin, operating profit margin, and net profit margin. Python's powerful data analysis libraries, such as Pandas and NumPy, allow for streamlined computation of these ratios.

For instance, to calculate the net profit margin:

python

```python
net_profit = 250000 # Replace with actual values
revenue = 1000000
net_profit_margin = (net_profit / revenue) * 100
```

Solvency Ratios

Solvency ratios assess a company's ability to meet its long-term obligations and remain financially stable in the long run. Debt to equity ratio, interest coverage ratio, and debt ratio are common solvency ratios. Python simplifies the data management and computations necessary for these ratios.

Calculating the debt to equity ratio using Python:

python

```
total_debt = 750000  # Replace with actual values
shareholders_equity = 1000000
debt_to_equity_ratio = total_debt / shareholders_equity
```

Efficiency Ratios

Efficiency ratios gauge how effectively a company utilizes its assets to generate sales and revenue. These ratios encompass inventory turnover, accounts receivable turnover, and asset turnover. Python's ability to handle vast datasets and automate calculations is a game-changer in computing efficiency ratios.

Automating the calculation of inventory turnover:

python

```
average_inventory = (beginning_inventory + ending_inventory) / 2  # Replace with actual values
cost_of_goods_sold = 500000
inventory_turnover = cost_of_goods_sold / average_inventory
```

Interpreting the Ratios

Python not only helps you compute these ratios but also visualize and interpret them effectively. Visualization libraries such as Matplotlib can be employed to create graphical representations of the ratios, making it easier for stakeholders to understand the financial health of the company.

Additionally, the Pandas library's data manipulation capabilities enable you to identify trends and anomalies in the financial data. By exploring historical financial data, you can use time series analysis techniques to predict future trends and make informed decisions. Python provides the tools for this analysis, allowing you to create financial forecasts and budgets accurately.

Time Series Analysis

Time series analysis is a powerful technique in the world of finance and accounting. It allows you to delve into historical data and uncover patterns, trends, and insights that can inform your decision-making process. In this section, we will explore the fascinating realm of time series analysis and how Python can be your trusted companion in this journey.

Understanding Time Series Data

Before we dive into the intricacies of time series analysis, it's crucial to understand what time series data is. Simply put, time series data is a sequence of data points collected, recorded, or measured at successive points in time. In finance and accounting, this could be daily stock prices, hourly sales figures, or monthly revenue data.

Time series data often exhibits a natural temporal ordering, making it ideal for studying trends, seasonality, and cyclic patterns. The ability to harness this data effectively can provide you with a competitive edge in various accounting tasks, from budgeting and forecasting to risk assessment.

Python's Role in Time Series Analysis

Python's popularity in financial analysis is not without reason. The language offers a wide array of libraries and tools that simplify the process of working with time series data. One of the most significant libraries in this context is Pandas, which provides extensive support for handling time series data structures.

Additionally, libraries like NumPy, Matplotlib, and Statsmodels can help you perform in-depth analysis, visualization, and forecasting on your financial data. Python's simplicity and versatility make it an ideal choice for both beginners and experienced analysts in the field of accounting.

Exploring Time Series Analysis Techniques

Data Preparation: The first step in time series analysis is data preparation. You'll need to load your historical data into Python, which can be stored in various formats such as CSV, Excel, or databases. Once loaded, Pandas can help you clean, resample, and manipulate the data to ensure it's in the right format for analysis.

python

# Sample code to load time series data using Pandas
import pandas as pd

# Load a CSV file
data = pd.read_csv('financial_data.csv')

Visualization: Visualizing your time series data is essential to identify any apparent trends, seasonality, or anomalies. Matplotlib, a popular Python library, allows you to create informative charts and graphs that can offer quick insights into your data.

python

```
# Sample code to create a time series plot
import matplotlib.pyplot as plt

# Plotting financial data
plt.plot(data, data)
plt.xlabel('Date')
plt.ylabel('Price')
plt.title('Financial Data Over Time')
plt.show()
```

Exploratory Data Analysis (EDA): EDA involves a more detailed examination of your data to uncover hidden patterns and relationships. Python libraries like Statsmodels and Seaborn provide tools for statistical analysis and advanced visualization.

python

```
# Sample code for EDA with Seaborn
import seaborn as sns

# Creating a pair plot for data exploration
sns.pairplot(data)
```

Time Series Decomposition: Time series data often comprises multiple components, including trends, seasonality, and noise. Python can help you decompose your data into these components, making it easier to analyze each part separately.

python

```python
# Sample code for time series decomposition
from statsmodels.tsa.seasonal import seasonal_decompose

# Decompose time series data
decomposition = seasonal_decompose(data, model='additive')
```

Time Series Forecasting: One of the primary goals of time series analysis is forecasting. Python offers numerous techniques for forecasting, such as ARIMA (AutoRegressive Integrated Moving Average), Exponential Smoothing, and machine learning models like LSTM (Long Short-Term Memory).

python

```python
# Sample code for time series forecasting with ARIMA
from statsmodels.tsa.arima_model import ARIMA

# Fit an ARIMA model to the data
model = ARIMA(data, order=(5,1,0))
results = model.fit()
```

Model Evaluation: After creating a forecast, it's essential to evaluate its accuracy. Python provides various metrics and tools for assessing how well your model performs.

python

```python
# Sample code for evaluating a forecasting model
from sklearn.metrics import mean_squared_error
```

```
# Calculate Mean Squared Error
mse = mean_squared_error(true_values, predicted_values)
```

Interpreting Financial Ratios

Now that we have a foundation in time series analysis using Python, let's connect this knowledge to the primary focus of this section: calculating financial ratios.

Financial ratios are critical for assessing a company's financial health, performance, and stability. In the context of time series analysis, you can utilize these ratios to evaluate how a company's financial position changes over time. Some essential financial ratios include:

Liquidity Ratios: These ratios measure a company's ability to meet short-term obligations. Examples include the current ratio and quick ratio.

Profitability Ratios: These ratios assess a company's ability to generate profits. Common ones include the net profit margin and return on equity.

Solvency Ratios: Solvency ratios determine a company's long-term financial stability. The debt-to-equity ratio is a notable example.

Efficiency Ratios: These ratios evaluate how efficiently a company manages its assets and liabilities. The inventory turnover ratio and accounts receivable turnover ratio fall into this category.

By calculating these ratios over time and applying time series analysis techniques, you can gain valuable insights into a company's financial trends. Are liquidity ratios improving or deteriorating? Is profitability on the rise? Are solvency ratios indicating stability?

In Python, Pandas and NumPy are your allies when working with financial data to calculate these ratios. Here's a brief example of calculating the current ratio:

python

```
# Sample code for calculating the current ratio
current_assets = data
current_liabilities = data
current_ratio = current_assets / current_liabilities
```

Remember that the interpretation of financial ratios should consider industry benchmarks and the company's specific circumstances.

By mastering the art of time series analysis in Python and pairing it with your knowledge of financial ratios, you'll be well-equipped to make informed decisions and provide valuable insights as an accountant. It's a skill set that can significantly enhance your role in any financial or accounting context.

Forecasting with Python:

Forecasting involves making predictions about future financial trends based on historical data. Python equips accountants with the necessary tools to create accurate forecasts. Let's consider an example:

Suppose you work for a retail company, and you want to forecast sales for the upcoming quarter. You have access to historical sales data, and with Python, you can employ various forecasting methods. One such method is time series forecasting, which uses historical data points to predict future values. The Python library, 'Prophet,' developed by Facebook, is a powerful tool for this purpose.

Here's a simplified Python code snippet that demonstrates time series forecasting using the 'Prophet' library:

python

```
# Importing necessary libraries
from fbprophet import Prophet
import pandas as pd

# Creating a DataFrame with historical sales data
data = pd.read_csv('sales_data.csv')

# Renaming columns to match Prophet's requirements
data = data.rename(columns={'Date': 'ds', 'Sales': 'y'})

# Creating a Prophet model
model = Prophet()

# Fitting the model to your data
model.fit(data)
```

```python
# Creating a DataFrame for future dates
future = model.make_future_dataframe(periods=90)

# Making predictions
forecast = model.predict(future)

# Visualizing the forecast
fig = model.plot(forecast)
```

This code snippet, while simplified, demonstrates the power of Python in forecasting. You can easily extend it to more complex scenarios, using additional variables and fine-tuning the model to improve forecast accuracy.

Budgeting with Python:

Budgeting is the process of creating a financial plan for an organization, setting income and expenditure targets, and ensuring financial goals are met. Python offers an excellent platform to streamline this process. Here's an example of using Python to create a budget for a project:

Let's say your organization is initiating a new project and you need to estimate the project's expenses. With Python, you can build a budgeting tool that takes various cost factors into account. Below is a basic Python script to calculate and present a project budget:

python

```python
# Define cost variables
```

```python
material_cost = 5000
labor_cost = 10000
equipment_cost = 3000
other_costs = 1500

# Calculate the total budget
total_budget = material_cost + labor_cost + equipment_cost + other_costs

# Display the budget breakdown
print("Project Budget Breakdown:")
print(f"Materials: ${material_cost}")
print(f"Labor: ${labor_cost}")
print(f"Equipment: ${equipment_cost}")
print(f"Other Costs: ${other_costs}")
print(f"Total Budget: ${total_budget}")
```

This simple Python script allows you to quickly calculate and visualize the budget for your project. It's easy to adjust variables and add more complexity to the budgeting process as needed.

The combination of time series forecasting and budgeting tools in Python equips accountants with powerful means to analyze financial data, predict future trends, and set up financial plans. This chapter guides you through the process of using Python for these tasks, ensuring you can make data-driven decisions and contribute to the financial health of your organization.

Through practical examples and hands-on exercises, you'll gain a deep understanding of financial forecasting and budgeting in Python. Remember, the key to successful forecasting and budgeting is a blend of historical data analysis, domain knowledge, and the tools Python provides. As you progress through this chapter, you'll become proficient in using Python for these crucial tasks, further enhancing your capabilities as an accountant. Whether you're in the corporate world, managing your own business, or working with clients, these skills are invaluable for informed decision-making and financial success.

Understanding Financial Risks

Before we plunge into the realm of Python-powered risk analysis, it's crucial to understand the nature of financial risks accountants face. Financial risks can manifest in various forms, including market risk, credit risk, operational risk, liquidity risk, and more. Each of these risks carries unique challenges, but collectively, they can impact an organization's stability and profitability.

Python: Your Risk Analysis Companion

Python's robust capabilities in data analysis, statistical modeling, and data visualization make it an ideal tool for tackling financial risks. Python's extensive libraries, such as NumPy, Pandas, and Scikit-Learn, empower accountants to work with financial data efficiently and implement advanced risk analysis techniques. Let's explore some key aspects of risk analysis that Python can assist with:

Risk Identification: The first step in risk analysis is identifying potential threats. Python can automate data collection and identify unusual patterns or outliers that may indicate underlying risks. By utilizing Pandas and Matplotlib, you can visualize data to spot anomalies more effectively.

Quantitative Risk Measurement: Once risks are identified, it's essential to quantify them. Python allows you to create advanced models for risk measurement, including Value at Risk (VaR) and Expected Shortfall (ES). These metrics provide insights into potential losses in adverse scenarios.

Monte Carlo Simulations: Python is well-known for its capacity to conduct Monte Carlo simulations. This technique involves creating thousands of possible scenarios to estimate the range of potential outcomes. Accountants can use these simulations to evaluate how different risks affect financial performance.

Stress Testing: Stress testing is crucial in assessing an organization's resilience to severe market shocks. Python's ability to handle large datasets and perform complex calculations makes it a valuable tool for stress testing various financial scenarios.

Risk Mitigation Strategies: Identifying risks is only part of the equation; mitigating them is equally important. Python can help you design strategies to manage risks, such as optimizing portfolios or developing hedging strategies using financial libraries like QuantLib-Python.

Python in Action: A Risk Analysis Example

Let's consider a scenario where a company has a diverse investment portfolio. The accountant needs to assess the portfolio's exposure to market risk and potential losses during turbulent times. Python can facilitate this process. By implementing historical data analysis, the accountant can use Python to calculate the portfolio's Value at Risk (VaR) and

HAYDEN VAN DER POST

identify the risk of substantial losses.

Here's a simplified Python code snippet to calculate VaR:

python

```python
import pandas as pd
import numpy as np
from scipy.stats import norm

# Input data: investment returns
returns = pd.Series()

# Calculate mean and standard deviation
mu = returns.mean()
sigma = returns.std()

# Define confidence level and time horizon
confidence_level = 0.95
time_horizon = 1

# Calculate VaR
z_score = norm.ppf(1 - (1 - confidence_level))
var = mu * time_horizon - z_score * sigma * np.sqrt(time_horizon)

print(f"Portfolio VaR at {confidence_level * 100}% confidence for {time_horizon}-day horizon: {var * 100:.2f}%")
```

This simple example demonstrates how Python can help

accountants estimate potential losses in their investment portfolio. In real-world scenarios, you would work with larger datasets and more complex models, but this code serves as a foundation for your risk analysis journey.

Risk analysis is a fundamental aspect of modern accounting, and Python is your trusted ally in this endeavor. Its versatility, data analysis capabilities, and vast library ecosystem empower accountants to not only identify and quantify risks but also devise effective mitigation strategies. By harnessing the power of Python, accountants can navigate the turbulent waters of financial risk with confidence and precision. Risk analysis is not just a tool; it's a mindset, and Python is your key to unlocking its potential in the world of accounting.

Practice Exercises and Case Study

In the realm of learning and mastering Python for accounting, we've arrived at a pivotal juncture in our journey – the application of financial analysis techniques through practice exercises and the examination of a real-world case study. The knowledge and skills you've gathered from previous chapters have primed you for this moment, where theory transforms into practical expertise.

The Power of Practice:

Practice makes perfect, or so the saying goes. This is no less true in the world of Python for accounting. As you delve into the practical exercises, you will have the opportunity to apply what you've learned. These exercises are designed to reinforce your understanding of financial analysis and how Python can be harnessed to unlock its full potential.

Let's begin by looking at a few example exercises and then transition to a comprehensive case study that ties all your knowledge together.

Exercise 1: Analyzing Financial Statements

Start with a simple exercise involving the analysis of financial statements. You'll be working with a sample dataset containing income statements and balance sheets for a fictional company. Your task is to calculate various financial ratios, such as the debt-to-equity ratio, current ratio, and net profit margin. Python allows you to automate these calculations and swiftly gain insights into the company's financial health.

Here's a Python code snippet that demonstrates the calculation of the debt-to-equity ratio:

python

```
# Sample financial data
total_debt = 1500000
total_equity = 2500000

# Calculate debt-to-equity ratio
debt_to_equity_ratio = total_debt / total_equity
print(f'Debt-to-Equity Ratio: {debt_to_equity_ratio:.2f}')
```

Exercise 2: Time Series Forecasting

The next exercise involves time series analysis and forecasting. Using historical sales data, you'll employ Python to create a time series model that predicts future sales. Time series analysis is critical in financial forecasting, and Python's libraries make it easier than ever. You'll explore methods like moving averages and exponential smoothing.

Below is an example code snippet for a simple moving average calculation:

python

```
# Sample sales data
sales_data =

# Calculate 3-month moving average
moving_average = sum(sales_data) / 3
print(f'3-Month Moving Average: {moving_average:.2f}')
```

Exercise 3: Risk Analysis

In this exercise, you'll work with a dataset containing historical stock prices for a set of companies. Your goal is to measure and analyze the risk associated with these stocks. Python's libraries will enable you to calculate metrics like standard deviation, beta, and Value at Risk (VaR). These metrics are essential for portfolio management and risk assessment.

Here's a Python code snippet for calculating the standard deviation of a stock's returns:

python

```
import numpy as np
```

```
# Sample stock returns
returns =

# Calculate standard deviation
std_deviation = np.std(returns)
print(f'Standard Deviation: {std_deviation:.4f}')
```

A Comprehensive Case Study: Bringing It All Together

After honing your skills through these practice exercises, it's time for a comprehensive case study. The case study provides you with an opportunity to consolidate your knowledge by tackling a real-world financial problem.

In this case study, you will dive into the world of investment portfolio analysis. Imagine you're an investment analyst responsible for optimizing a client's investment portfolio. You have historical data for various stocks, and your goal is to construct a portfolio that maximizes returns while minimizing risk.

This case study will involve:

Data cleaning and preprocessing: Handling missing data and outliers in the stock data.

Risk assessment: Calculating key risk metrics for each stock.

Portfolio optimization: Creating an optimal portfolio allocation based on your risk-return preferences.

Performance evaluation: Measuring the performance of your portfolio against relevant benchmarks.

By the end of this case study, you'll be well-versed in the practical application of Python for financial analysis, and you'll have a powerful portfolio optimization tool at your disposal.

Conclusion

Chapter 3 Has Been An Exciting Journey, Introducing You To The Core Principles Of Python For Accounting. We've Covered Everything From Understanding Financial Statements And Calculating Ratios To Delving Into Time Series Analysis And Risk Assessment. You've Laid The Foundation For Robust Financial Analysis And Have Practical Python Skills At Your Fingertips.

Now, as you embark on Chapter 4, you'll discover how Python can be your ally in automating repetitive tasks and ensuring the integrity of your financial data. Join us in Chapter 4 as we explore "Automation and Efficiency," where you'll learn how to streamline your accounting processes and ensure data accuracy with the power of Python. The road ahead is filled with opportunities for greater efficiency and precision in your accounting endeavors.

CHAPTER 4: AUTOMATION AND EFFICIENCY

In the world of accounting, efficiency is paramount. Accountants and financial professionals often find themselves engaged in repetitive, time-consuming tasks that can be automated to free up valuable time and reduce the risk of human error. This is where Python comes into play as a powerful tool for automating these repetitive tasks, allowing accountants to focus on more complex and strategic aspects of their work.

Why Automation Matters

Before delving into Python's capabilities for automation, it's crucial to understand why automating repetitive tasks is a game-changer in the realm of accounting. Automation matters for several reasons:

1. Time Savings: One of the most immediate benefits of automation is the time it saves. Tasks that would typically take hours or even days to complete manually can be done in a matter of minutes using Python scripts.

2. Error Reduction: Automation significantly reduces the risk of

errors. Humans are prone to making mistakes, especially when performing monotonous, repetitive tasks. Automation ensures consistency and accuracy in data handling.

3. Enhanced Productivity: By automating repetitive tasks, accountants can allocate more time to tasks that require their expertise and decision-making, ultimately boosting overall productivity.

4. Cost Efficiency: With increased efficiency, organizations can reduce labor costs and reallocate resources to other strategic areas.

5. Data Quality: Automated processes ensure that data is processed consistently and is of high quality. This leads to more reliable financial reports and insights.

Python's Role in Automation

Python is celebrated for its versatility, making it an ideal choice for automating various tasks in accounting. Here's how it plays a pivotal role in streamlining processes:

1. Data Entry and Validation: Python scripts can be developed to automate the input and validation of data. For instance, data from various sources can be imported, cleaned, and integrated seamlessly into accounting systems. The scripts can include checks to ensure data accuracy and integrity.

2. Reporting: Generating financial reports is a common and repetitive task in accounting. With Python, accountants can create scripts to generate customized reports automatically. This includes income statements, balance sheets, and other financial reports tailored to specific requirements.

3. Data Transformation: Many accounting processes require data transformation, such as currency conversion or unit adjustments. Python can handle these tasks with ease, ensuring consistency and accuracy.

4. Billing and Invoicing: Automation of billing and invoicing is another area where Python shines. It can create and send invoices to clients and vendors based on predefined criteria, reducing the need for manual input.

Designing Python Scripts for Automation

When automating repetitive accounting tasks using Python, it's essential to follow a structured approach:

1. Identify Repetitive Tasks: Begin by identifying the tasks that consume a significant amount of time and are prone to human error. These are prime candidates for automation.

2. Define Clear Objectives: Clearly define the objectives of the automation process. What is the expected outcome? What data needs to be processed, and in what format?

3. Develop Python Scripts: Python offers a wide range of libraries and tools that can be leveraged for automation. For instance, if you are automating data entry, you might use libraries like Pandas for data manipulation and PyInput for data entry. Python scripts should be well-documented for future reference.

4. Testing and Validation: Before deploying any automation process, thoroughly test the Python scripts to ensure they function correctly. Validate the results and check for any

discrepancies.

5. Implement Error Handling: It's essential to include error-handling mechanisms in your Python scripts. This ensures that if an unexpected issue arises, the script can respond appropriately and provide notifications if necessary.

6. Monitor and Maintain: Even after automation, it's crucial to monitor the processes and maintain the scripts. Accounting practices evolve, and data sources may change, so ongoing maintenance is essential.

Case Study: Streamlining Invoice Generation

Let's consider a practical example. An accounting firm regularly sends invoices to clients based on billable hours. Using Python, they've automated the process. Here's how it works:

The Python script retrieves billable hour data from the firm's database.

It generates invoices for each client, calculating the total amount based on hourly rates.

The script sends the invoices via email to clients as PDF attachments.

As a result, the firm has not only saved countless hours but also reduced errors related to invoicing. The clients receive their invoices promptly, leading to improved client satisfaction.

The Road to Efficiency

Automation is not just a trend; it's the future of accounting. By adopting Python and leveraging its capabilities, accountants can streamline their workflows, save time, enhance data accuracy, and focus on higher-value tasks. Automation is the road to efficiency, and Python is the vehicle that will take accountants there. In the next section, we'll delve into another aspect of automation: the implementation of audit trails to ensure financial data integrity. This ensures that every change or entry in your accounting data is traceable and accountable. It's an essential component of maintaining the quality and trustworthiness of your financial records.

But before we continue, remember that the key to successful automation is identifying the right tasks to automate, and understanding the tools and libraries available in Python to accomplish those tasks. So, let's embark on the journey of automating your accounting tasks with Python, paving the way for a more efficient and productive future.

Using Python for Audit Trail

In this pivotal section, we delve into the world of financial data integrity and accountability, exploring the critical concept of an audit trail and how Python can be your trusted companion in maintaining it.

Ensuring Data Integrity

In the realm of accounting, data integrity is a non-negotiable aspect. A small error or discrepancy can have significant consequences, making it imperative to ensure that your financial data is not tampered with. This is where implementing an audit trail becomes essential.

The Audit Trail Unveiled

An audit trail is essentially a chronological record of every change made to financial data. This record reveals who made the change, what change was made, and when the change occurred. The purpose of an audit trail is to provide a clear and tamper-evident history of financial transactions and data manipulations.

With Python, the creation and management of an audit trail can be streamlined and automated, saving you time and mitigating risks associated with manual record-keeping. This section explores how to leverage Python for this very purpose.

Python's Role in the Audit Trail

Python offers a variety of libraries and tools to facilitate the establishment of a robust audit trail. Here, we'll take a closer look at how Python can help you implement this crucial process.

Traceability: Python enables you to track every change made to your financial data. When a modification is made, Python records it with detailed information, making it easy to trace back to the source of any alteration.

Accountability: It's vital to know who is responsible for each data modification. Python allows you to associate changes with specific s, creating a transparent record of accountability.

Tamper Resistance: One of the key benefits of using Python for an audit trail is its ability to resist tampering. With the right implementation, Python can ensure that once a record is created, it cannot be altered or deleted without detection.

An Illustration with Python

To better understand the practicality of Python in maintaining an audit trail, let's walk through a simple example. We'll consider a scenario where you're managing financial transactions for a small business, and you want to track any changes made to the financial records.

python

```
# Example Python code for implementing an audit trail

# Import required libraries
import datetime

# Define a function to log changes
def log_change(, action, amount):
    timestamp = datetime.datetime.now()
    log_entry = f"{timestamp} - {} {action} ${amount}"

    # Append the log entry to a file
    with open("audit_log.txt", "a") as log_file:
        log_file.write(log_entry + "\n")

# Simulate a transaction
= "John"
action = "added"
amount = 1000
log_change(, action, amount)
```

In this Python code, we create a function log_change() that takes parameters for the , action, and the transaction amount. It then appends a log entry to an audit trail file, which records the timestamp, , action, and amount.

Setting Up Python for Audit Trails

As you venture into using Python for audit trails, we'll explore not only the code examples but also the best practices for maintaining a secure and efficient audit trail system. This includes considerations for log file storage, access controls, and more.

By the end of this section, you'll have a deep understanding of how to use Python for implementing an audit trail that ensures the integrity of your financial data and provides a clear path to accountability. You'll be well-equipped to deploy this knowledge into your accounting processes, creating a secure environment for financial transactions.

Now that we've delved into the world of audit trails, Chapter 4 opens up the next dimension in our journey, focusing on "Streamlining Reporting." We'll explore how to efficiently create and automate financial reports using Python, reducing manual effort and increasing accuracy. Join us in Chapter 4 as we explore this transformative facet of Python for accountants.

Efficient Reporting Techniques

Efficiency in financial reporting is essential. As an accountant, you'll often find yourself dealing with a large volume of data, and manually generating reports can be time-consuming and prone to errors. Python offers a host of libraries that can significantly expedite this process. One such library is "Pandas," which is widely regarded for its data manipulation capabilities.

Pandas allows you to read, clean, and transform data with ease. You can quickly import data from various sources, such as CSV files, databases, or APIs, making it adaptable to different accounting systems. Its ability to handle missing values and outliers ensures the data you report is accurate.

To give you a glimpse of the power of Pandas in reporting, let's consider an example. Imagine you're tasked with generating a monthly financial report for your company. In a traditional approach, you'd need to manually extract data from multiple sources, clean it, and aggregate the information into a readable format. With Pandas, you can automate these tasks.

python

```python
import pandas as pd

# Load data from CSV
data = pd.read_csv('financial_data.csv')

# Data cleaning and transformation
data = data.dropna() # Handling missing values
data = data < 10000] # Handling outliers

# Aggregating data for reporting
monthly_report = data.groupby('month').sum()
```

The above code loads financial data from a CSV file, cleans it by removing missing values and outliers, and aggregates it to create a monthly financial report. This entire process, which would take hours manually, can be executed in a matter of seconds with Python.

Automation of Financial Reporting Processes

While Pandas is a crucial component of efficient reporting, Python's automation capabilities extend beyond data manipulation. With libraries like "OpenPyXL" for working with Excel files or "ReportLab" for creating PDF reports, you can automate the generation of visually appealing reports.

Let's look at an example that demonstrates how Python can automate the creation of financial statements in an Excel workbook:

python

```python
import openpyxl

# Load an Excel template
wb = openpyxl.load_workbook('financial_template.xlsx')
sheet = wb

# Update the balance sheet with new data
sheet = '2023-03-31'
sheet = 250000 # New total assets
sheet = 175000 # New total liabilities

# Save the updated workbook
wb.save('financial_statement_2023.xlsx')
```

In this example, we open an existing Excel template, update the balance sheet with the latest figures, and save it as a new report. Such automation ensures that your financial statements are always up to date with minimal manual effort.

Automation also reduces the likelihood of errors that can creep in when generating reports manually. Consistency in formatting and calculations is maintained, improving the quality and reliability of your financial reports.

By streamlining reporting with Python, you not only save time but also improve the accuracy and efficiency of your financial reporting processes. With the right libraries and tools at your disposal, you can transform reporting from a laborious task into a strategic asset for your accounting practice.

In the next section, we'll explore how to schedule and automate the execution of Python scripts for various accounting tasks using tools like "cron jobs." This will further enhance the efficiency of your accounting operation.

Task Scheduling and Cron Jobs

In the fast-paced world of accounting, efficiency is the name of the game. With a wealth of financial data to process and reports to generate, it's essential to automate repetitive tasks to free up valuable time for more strategic activities. In this section, we dive into the realm of task scheduling and explore the potent tool known as the cron job scheduler.

Automating Repetitive Tasks with Python

Python's versatility extends beyond data analysis and reporting; it can also serve as your trusty automation companion. With automation, you can delegate tasks such as data entry, report generation, and data processing to Python scripts. But how can you ensure these tasks run reliably and consistently without manual intervention? This is where task scheduling comes into play.

Understanding Task Scheduling

Task scheduling is the art of automating the execution of scripts, programs, or tasks at specified intervals or times. It's like having an assistant that performs repetitive tasks for you without fail. In the context of Python, you can schedule the execution of your Python scripts to run at designated times or intervals.

Python offers various ways to schedule tasks, such as using built-in libraries like time or third-party libraries like schedule. However, one of the most commonly used tools for task scheduling in the UNIX-like operating systems is the cron job scheduler.

Meet Cron: Your Time-Triggered Assistant

Cron, short for "chronograph," is a time-based job scheduler in Unix-like operating systems. It allows you to schedule tasks to run at specified times or intervals automatically. With cron, you can schedule Python scripts to execute daily, weekly, monthly, or at specific times during the day. This level of control is indispensable for automating routine accounting processes.

Here's a glimpse of how you can use cron to schedule Python scripts:

Setting the Schedule: You define when and how often you want a script to run. For example, you can schedule a script to run every day at 2:00 PM.

Choosing the Python Interpreter: You specify the Python interpreter to use. This is particularly important if you're working with virtual environments.

Selecting the Script: You point to the Python script you want to run.

Redirection and Logging: You can redirect the script's output to a file, making it easy to review and troubleshoot later.

Practical Applications in Accounting

Now, let's explore some practical applications of task scheduling in accounting:

Regular Report Generation: You can schedule Python scripts to generate daily, weekly, or monthly financial reports. These reports can be automatically emailed to relevant stakeholders.

Data Backup: Automate the process of creating backups for critical financial data. Scheduled backups ensure data security and availability.

Data Retrieval: Retrieve financial data from various sources at specific intervals. For instance, you can fetch exchange rates daily to keep currency conversions up to date.

Data Processing: If you need to process financial data received at a particular time each day, you can schedule data processing scripts to run automatically.

Python and Cron: A Perfect Pair

The synergy between Python and cron is remarkable. Python is known for its ease of use and extensive libraries, while cron adds the element of time-based automation. This pairing enables accountants to streamline their workflows and enhance productivity.

Let's consider an example to illustrate how Python and cron can work together in an accounting scenario. Suppose you work for a retail business, and you need to update the sales data on a daily basis. Here's how you can automate this task:

Python Script: You write a Python script that retrieves the latest sales data from the database.

Cron Job: You schedule this Python script to run every day at midnight, ensuring that it captures the sales data for the entire day.

Data Processing: The script processes the data, updating the sales records, and generating daily sales reports.

Notification: If the script encounters any issues, you can set it up to send an email notification.

Anatomy of a Cron Job

A cron job consists of two main parts: the schedule and the command. The schedule is defined using five asterisks, indicating the minute, hour, day of the month, month, and day of the week when the task should run. The command is the actual task you want to execute.

Here's a sample cron job entry:

ruby

0 0 * * * /usr/bin/python3 /path/to/your_script.py

In this example, the script is scheduled to run at midnight every day.

Final Thoughts

Task scheduling with Python and cron is an indispensable tool in the accountant's toolbox. It empowers you to automate repetitive tasks, thereby reducing the risk of errors and freeing your time for more strategic activities. With the ability to set precise schedules, you can trust that your critical accounting processes are executed reliably.

The Role of Error Handling

In the previous section, you've learned how to automate repetitive accounting tasks, streamline reporting, and manage data integrity. Yet, in the world of programming, errors are inevitable. These errors can manifest in various forms, from syntax errors to unexpected data issues, and they can disrupt your automated processes if not handled correctly.

Error handling is like having a safety net that prevents your Python scripts from crashing when they encounter unforeseen problems. In the context of Python for accounting, this safety net is a critical aspect of ensuring data accuracy and the reliability of automated accounting processes.

Types of Errors in Python

Before delving into error handling, it's essential to understand the types of errors you might encounter in your Python scripts:

Syntax Errors: These occur when you've violated the rules of Python's syntax. For example, if you forget to close a parenthesis, you'll encounter a syntax error.

Runtime Errors: Also known as exceptions, these errors happen during the execution of your code. Common examples include trying to access a non-existent file or dividing by zero.

Logic Errors: These are the trickiest to spot because they don't trigger error messages. Instead, your code runs, but it doesn't produce the expected output due to flawed logic.

Error Handling in Python

Python provides a robust error-handling mechanism that allows you to anticipate potential errors and respond to them gracefully. The primary tools for handling errors in Python are the "try" and "except" blocks. Here's how they work:

python

```
try:
    # Code that may cause an error
    result = 10 / 0
except ZeroDivisionError:
    # Code to handle the error
```

```python
    print("You can't divide by zero.")
```

In the code above, Python attempts to execute the division operation, but if a ZeroDivisionError occurs (i.e., division by zero), it gracefully handles the error by printing a customized message.

The Importance of Customized Error Messages

When working on accounting automation scripts, creating custom error messages is paramount. Rather than presenting generic error messages, you can provide specific information about the nature of the error and potential solutions. For example:

python

```python
try:
    # Code that may cause an error
    result = some_function()
except FileNotFoundError:
    # Customized error message
    print("The specified file is missing. Please check the file path.")
```

Customized error messages not only make troubleshooting easier for you but also for any colleagues or s who may interact with your scripts in the future.

Setting Up Notifications

While handling errors effectively is crucial, being proactive in notifying relevant stakeholders about errors is equally important. In automated accounting processes, a delay in addressing an issue could have significant consequences. Notifications can be in the form of email alerts, log entries, or messages to a designated channel.

Here's an example of sending an email notification when an error occurs:

python

```
import smtplib

try:
    # Code that may cause an error
    result = perform_critical_operation()
except Exception as e:
    # Notify relevant parties about the error
    error_message = f"An error occurred: {str(e)}"
    send_email("accounting@example.com", "Error    Alert", error_message)
```

In the code above, when an error occurs, it captures the error message and sends an email to the specified address, providing immediate notification.

Practice Exercises and Case Study

In the world of accounting, the ability to automate repetitive tasks and streamline processes is nothing short of a superpower. Imagine the time and effort saved by harnessing the immense potential of Python for automation. This chapter delves deep into practical exercises and presents a compelling case study to illustrate how Python can transform the way accountants work.

Automation is all about efficiency and precision. By reducing manual intervention and minimizing the scope for human error, Python plays a pivotal role in reshaping accounting practices. In this section, we'll explore some practical exercises that not only highlight the power of automation but also offer hands-on experience for readers.

Practice Exercise 1: Streamlining Data Entry

One of the most laborious tasks in accounting is entering data from various sources into the accounting system. Python can be your best ally in this endeavor. Let's consider a scenario where you receive financial data in the form of CSV files from multiple departments. Manually entering this data is not only tedious but also prone to errors.

With Python, you can write scripts to automate the data entry process. You can use libraries like Pandas to read data from CSV files, perform necessary data transformations, and insert it directly into your accounting software. This not only saves time but also ensures data accuracy. Let's take a look at a Python code snippet to automate this process:

python

```
import pandas as pd

# Read data from CSV file
data = pd.read_csv('financial_data.csv')
```

```
# Perform data transformations as required
# ...
```

```
# Insert data into the accounting system
# ...
```

This exercise allows you to experience the power of Python in streamlining data entry tasks.

Generating financial reports is a critical part of an accountant's role. However, it can be time-consuming, especially when you need to prepare reports on a regular basis. Python can automate the entire reporting process. By writing scripts that extract data, perform necessary calculations, and create formatted reports, you can significantly reduce the time spent on this repetitive task.

Here's a simplified example of how Python can be used to generate financial reports:

python

```
# Extract financial data from accounting software
data = extract_data()
```

```
# Perform calculations for the report
calculations = perform_calculations(data)
```

```
# Create and format the report
generate_report(calculations)
```

By mastering these exercises, you'll be equipped with the skills needed to revolutionize the way data is managed and reported in your accounting work. It's not just about efficiency; it's about precision and reliability.

Case Study: Streamlined Accounting Processes

To truly appreciate the impact of automation and efficiency in accounting, let's dive into a real-world case study. Imagine a medium-sized manufacturing company dealing with thousands of transactions daily. Their accounting team was overwhelmed with manual data entry and report generation tasks. Errors were creeping in, and deadlines were frequently missed.

This is where Python stepped in as the hero of the story. The company hired a Python-savvy accountant who designed a comprehensive automation system. Data from various departments was now collected in a central repository, thanks to Python scripts that extracted, transformed, and loaded the data seamlessly. Human errors were drastically reduced.

The reporting process was also revolutionized. Python scripts were written to generate daily, weekly, and monthly financial reports automatically. These reports were not only generated on time but also came with an added layer of insights, thanks to Python's data analysis capabilities.

The case study showcases the tangible benefits of implementing Python for automation in accounting. By embracing automation, the accounting team was not only able to meet deadlines consistently but also had more time for strategic financial analysis and decision-making.

The combination of the practical exercises and the real-life case study demonstrates the immense potential of Python in automating and streamlining accounting processes. As you delve deeper into the world of Python, you'll discover that it's not just a tool but a transformational force that can elevate your accounting practices to new heights. The true power of Python lies in its ability to unlock efficiency, precision, and strategic thinking in the realm of accounting.

Conclusion

In accounting, efficiency is the cornerstone of success. With Python as your partner, the possibilities for automation and streamlining are endless. By embracing automation in data entry, report generation, and countless other tasks, you unlock newfound precision and time for strategic thinking.

As you've journeyed through this chapter, you've not only learned about the potential of Python but also witnessed its practical application through exercises and a compelling case study. But remember, this is just the beginning.

In Chapter 5, we delve into "Advanced topics in Python for Accounting," where you'll explore the art of turning raw financial data into meaningful insights and compelling visualizations. Get ready to uncover the data's stories and learn how Python can be your lens into the world of numbers.

CHAPTER 5: ADVANCED TOPICS IN PYTHON FOR ACCOUNTING

Welcome to Chapter 5, where we delve into the advanced realms of Python's applications in the field of accounting. This chapter is a thrilling expedition into the sophisticated tools and techniques that Python offers to revolutionize accounting practices.

Throughout your exploration in this chapter, you'll uncover the potential of Python for complex financial forecasting. Leveraging machine learning algorithms, we'll explore precise financial forecasts and predictive models that can take your analysis to the next level.

But our exploration doesn't stop there. We'll navigate the fascinating world of Natural Language Processing (NLP) for text analysis. Discover how you can extract valuable insights from textual financial data, providing a new dimension to your analytical capabilities.

This chapter also ventures into the world of blockchain and cryptocurrency accounting, a rapidly evolving field with unique challenges. You'll learn how Python can assist in handling cryptocurrency transactions and understanding their tax implications.

Integration with existing accounting software is a key focus. Streamlining data transfer and analysis is essential for increased efficiency, and Python offers innovative solutions in this area.

To ensure you're always at the forefront of accounting technology, we'll explore emerging trends and innovations, preparing you for the future.

Machine Learning for Forecasting

Machine learning is at the forefront of data-driven decision-making, and its applications in accounting are profound. The ability to forecast financial outcomes with greater accuracy is a game-changer, allowing businesses and financial professionals to make informed decisions. But before we delve into the intricacies of building predictive models, let's understand the fundamental concepts.

The Essence of Machine Learning

Machine learning is about teaching computers to recognize patterns in data. In the context of financial forecasting, this means using historical financial data to train a machine learning model. The model learns from the past to predict future financial trends.

We often use a type of machine learning called "supervised learning." This means we provide the model with historical data, including both the input variables (financial parameters) and the desired output (what we want to predict). For instance, you might feed the model with years of financial statements and their corresponding outcomes, like profit or loss.

The model learns the relationships within the data, allowing it to make predictions. These predictions can include anything from stock prices to future revenue or expense trends. The power of machine learning lies in its ability to consider numerous variables simultaneously, making it far more complex and accurate than traditional methods.

Building Predictive Models

To build predictive models in Python, you'll primarily rely on libraries such as scikit-learn and TensorFlow. These libraries offer a wide range of machine learning algorithms and tools that simplify the process. Let's take a simplified example to illustrate the concept.

Imagine you want to predict a company's future quarterly revenue based on historical data. You'd begin by collecting the relevant historical financial data, which might include variables such as marketing spend, number of employees, previous revenue, and more. With this data, you'll:

Data Preparation: Prepare your data by cleaning it, handling missing values, and scaling features. This step is crucial for the model to learn effectively.

Feature Selection: Choose the most relevant features (variables) that have the most impact on the target variable, which is your revenue prediction.

Model Selection: Select an appropriate machine learning algorithm. For regression tasks like revenue prediction, you'd opt for regression algorithms, such as linear regression or support vector regression.

Training the Model: Feed your historical data into the chosen algorithm. The model will learn the patterns and relationships within the data.

Evaluation and Fine-Tuning: Evaluate the model's performance using metrics like Mean Squared Error (MSE) or R-squared. Fine-tune the model parameters to improve accuracy.

Prediction: Once your model is trained and validated, you can use it to make future predictions. Input the relevant parameters, and the model will provide you with the forecasted revenue.

It's essential to understand that building effective machine learning models is a science and an art. It involves experimentation, iteration, and continuous improvement. Python's rich ecosystem of libraries, combined with the vast community of data scientists and developers, provides ample resources to support your journey.

Beyond the Basics

Machine learning goes far beyond simple regression models. You can explore advanced techniques like time series forecasting, ensemble methods, and deep learning for more complex predictions. Additionally, you'll discover how machine learning can assist in anomaly detection, risk assessment, and portfolio optimization—integral components of advanced financial analysis.

In this chapter, we'll provide practical examples of building machine learning models for various financial scenarios. You'll work with real datasets and Python code, allowing you to gain hands-on experience in leveraging machine learning for precise financial forecasts.

By the end of Chapter 5, you'll be well-equipped to harness the full potential of machine learning in accounting. Whether you're predicting financial trends, optimizing investment strategies, or identifying outliers in your data, machine learning will become a valuable ally in your journey. Get ready to dive into this exciting world of predictive power.

Natural Language Processing (NLP) for Text Analysis

In the vast landscape of accounting, numbers reign supreme. But buried beneath the numeric facade are extensive textual documents, financial reports, legal filings, and correspondence that hold valuable insights. The application of Natural Language Processing (NLP) in accounting is akin to transforming uncharted territory into a goldmine of information.

Unearthing Insights from Textual Data

We've spent considerable time understanding the world of numbers, algorithms, and forecasts. Now, let's delve into a domain where words matter just as much. NLP, a subfield of artificial intelligence, empowers us to process and comprehend human language, making it a powerful tool for interpreting financial texts.

The Textual Treasury

Think about the multitude of textual data that engulfs financial institutions daily. From lengthy annual reports to transaction descriptions, from customer feedback to legal documents, there's a wealth of untapped information. This is where NLP enters the scene, with the ability to automate the analysis of this textual treasury.

Syntax and Semantics

NLP operates on two fundamental levels: syntax and semantics. Syntax deals with the structure of language, such as sentence construction and grammar. Semantics, on the other hand, focuses on the meaning of words and the context in which they are used. These two pillars enable NLP to decipher the intricacies of textual data.

Application in Accounting

NLP in accounting is not just a trend; it's a necessity. Consider the applications:

Sentiment Analysis: By analyzing the sentiment of customer feedback or employee comments, you can gauge customer satisfaction and employee morale, which directly impact financial performance.

Risk Assessment: NLP can scan legal documents and news reports to identify potential legal risks or market developments, providing early warnings that are crucial for financial planning.

Fraud Detection: Unusual language patterns or discrepancies in textual data can be early signs of fraudulent activities. NLP can flag such anomalies for further investigation.

Financial Reports: Extracting relevant information from financial reports, SEC filings, or earnings call transcripts can automate data entry and trend analysis.

Regulatory Compliance: NLP can help ensure that financial documents meet the requirements of regulatory bodies by scanning for specific terms or clauses.

Tax Compliance: It can identify key financial data in unstructured text and cross-verify it with tax regulations, reducing the risk of non-compliance.

Practical Implementation

The power of NLP lies in its versatility. Let's illustrate its application in a financial context:

Example 1: Sentiment Analysis

Imagine you're a financial analyst assessing a publicly traded company. You have access to years of quarterly earnings call transcripts. Instead of reading through them manually, NLP can automatically analyze and categorize the sentiment expressed by the company's management during these calls. Positive sentiments might indicate confidence and growth, while negative sentiments could suggest issues that may impact stock prices.

Example 2: Regulatory Compliance

When preparing financial reports, compliance with SEC regulations is paramount. NLP can automatically check the reports for all the required clauses, making sure they're included and that the wording complies with the guidelines. This not only saves time but also reduces the risk of non-compliance.

Example 3: Tax Compliance

For a large corporation, tax compliance is an intricate process.

Contracts, agreements, and financial documents are filled with information relevant to tax calculations. NLP can swiftly extract the necessary data, cross-reference it with tax regulations, and ensure that every detail is considered.

Tools of the Trade

NLP tools and libraries, such as NLTK, spaCy, and Gensim, have made their mark in the world of text analysis. Python, our trusty companion, offers numerous packages that seamlessly integrate NLP into your accounting workflow. These tools provide pre-trained models and customizable pipelines for tasks like named entity recognition, sentiment analysis, and text summarization.

Real-World Applications

The world of finance is continuously evolving, and NLP is at the forefront of this transformation. Investment banks use NLP to scour news articles and social media for market-moving information. Hedge funds employ it to gain an edge in algorithmic trading. Accounting firms harness its power for auditing and risk management.

In Python, as Always

Here's the moment we've been waiting for. Python, with its extensive libraries like NLTK and spaCy, is your gateway to the world of NLP. Let's dive into a simple Python code example to illustrate how you can perform sentiment analysis using NLP:

```python
import nltk
from nltk.sentiment.vader import SentimentIntensityAnalyzer

# Initialize the sentiment analyzer
```

```python
analyzer = SentimentIntensityAnalyzer()

# Sample text
text = "The company's quarterly earnings exceeded
expectations, driving stock prices up."

# Analyze sentiment
sentiment = analyzer.polarity_scores(text)

# Interpret the sentiment scores
if sentiment >= 0.05:
    print("Positive sentiment")
elif sentiment <= -0.05:
    print("Negative sentiment")
else:
    print("Neutral sentiment")
```

This code uses the VADER sentiment analysis tool from the NLTK library to assess the sentiment of a given text. It calculates a compound score and classifies the sentiment as positive, negative, or neutral based on this score.

The union of Python, NLP, and accounting widens the horizons for understanding and utilizing financial data. As you journey further into the world of Python for accounting, remember that the language of numbers is not the only language worth mastering.

Blockchain and Cryptocurrency Accounting

The financial landscape has undergone a significant transformation with the emergence of blockchain technology and the rise of cryptocurrencies. These digital assets, which include Bitcoin, Ethereum, and many others, have introduced new challenges and opportunities to the world of accounting. In this chapter, we will explore the complexities of blockchain and cryptocurrency accounting and how Python can be leveraged to navigate this evolving landscape.

Understanding Blockchain and Cryptocurrency

Blockchain, the technology behind cryptocurrencies, is a decentralized and distributed ledger system that records all transactions across a network. Each transaction is grouped into a block, and a chain is formed as new blocks are added, creating an immutable record of all transactions. The security and transparency of blockchain have made it a popular choice for various financial transactions, including the creation and exchange of cryptocurrencies.

Cryptocurrencies, on the other hand, are digital or virtual currencies that use cryptography for security. They are not controlled by any central authority, such as a government or bank. The decentralized nature of cryptocurrencies has led to their adoption for various purposes, including online purchases, investments, and as a means of transferring value globally.

Challenges in Cryptocurrency Accounting

Accounting for traditional assets like cash, stocks, or real estate is well-established and follows standardized principles. However, cryptocurrency accounting introduces unique challenges. These include:

Price Volatility: Cryptocurrency values can fluctuate dramatically in a short period. This volatility complicates the valuation of assets and the calculation of profits and losses.

Multiple Transactions: Cryptocurrency transactions can involve multiple parties and addresses, making it complex to track and reconcile these transactions.

Lack of Regulation: The absence of uniform regulatory guidelines in the cryptocurrency space adds to the complexity of accounting practices.

Security Concerns: Protecting digital wallets and private keys is crucial, as the loss or theft of these can result in significant financial losses.

How Python Simplifies Cryptocurrency Accounting

Python is a versatile programming language that offers a range of libraries and tools for managing cryptocurrency-related tasks. Here are some key ways Python can simplify cryptocurrency accounting:

Data Retrieval: Python can connect to various cryptocurrency exchanges and blockchain networks to fetch transaction data, including transaction history and wallet balances. Libraries like ccxt provide a unified interface for interacting with multiple exchanges.

Data Parsing and Analysis: Python's data manipulation and analysis libraries, such as Pandas, make it easy to parse and analyze transaction data. You can track inflows and outflows, calculate gains and losses, and generate reports for tax purposes.

Security: Python allows for secure management of private keys and wallet addresses. You can create scripts to automate wallet management while maintaining robust security practices.

Tax Reporting: Python can help automate the generation of tax reports by calculating capital gains or losses based on your transaction history.

Tax Implications of Cryptocurrency

Handling the tax implications of cryptocurrency transactions is a crucial aspect of cryptocurrency accounting. Depending on your jurisdiction, the tax treatment of cryptocurrencies may vary. Common tax events related to cryptocurrencies include capital gains, income from mining, and taxable events like trading or spending cryptocurrency.

Python can assist with tax reporting by creating scripts that classify transactions, calculate tax obligations, and generate necessary reports for tax authorities. Additionally, Python scripts can keep records of historical prices, which is essential for calculating capital gains.

Conclusion

Blockchain and cryptocurrency accounting present accountants and financial professionals with a unique set of challenges. However, with the right tools and knowledge, these challenges can be effectively managed. Python's versatility and extensive libraries make it a valuable asset in simplifying cryptocurrency accounting tasks.

Integration with Accounting Software

Imagine having the ability to seamlessly connect your Python-powered data analysis and manipulation with your existing accounting software. The efficiency gains from such integration are nothing short of revolutionary. This section explores how to integrate Python solutions into your accounting processes, making them more efficient and hassle-free.

The Power of Integration

Accounting software is a staple in the modern financial world. These tools handle everything from bookkeeping to tax calculations, making accountants' lives much easier. Yet, there are situations where out-of-the-box solutions fall short. Python, with its adaptability, can bridge these gaps.

Python's Flexibility

One of Python's standout characteristics is its flexibility. This makes it a prime candidate for integration. No matter your accounting software of choice—be it QuickBooks, Xero, or any other—the power to enhance and streamline your operations lies in Python's capacity to interface with a variety of systems.

Consider a scenario where you're managing multiple clients with different accounting software preferences. Python can act as the unifying force, extracting data from these systems, and allowing you to analyze them collectively. This can lead to more comprehensive insights and improved client services.

APIs and Python

Most modern accounting software platforms provide Application Programming Interfaces (APIs) to facilitate communication with external systems. Python can harness these APIs to extract, manipulate, and transfer data. This integration can be instrumental in handling diverse financial data sources or automating routine tasks.

Example: Integrating with QuickBooks

Let's explore a common integration example: connecting Python with QuickBooks. This process requires several steps:

Set Up Developer Account: You'll need to create a developer account with QuickBooks and access your API keys.

OAuth 2.0 Authentication: Implement OAuth 2.0 to establish a secure connection between Python and QuickBooks.

API Requests: Utilize Python libraries such as requests or specialized QuickBooks libraries to send requests to the QuickBooks API. You can fetch transaction data, customer details, or anything else available via the API.

Data Processing: Python allows you to process the received data efficiently. You can perform complex calculations, create custom reports, or manipulate data as needed.

Data Transfer: With your data processed and analyzed, you can transfer it back to QuickBooks or any other accounting software you're working with.

The Magic of Data Analysis

Once you've integrated Python with your accounting software, the real magic begins. You can automate repetitive tasks, generate customized financial reports, and perform advanced analytics. For example, you can:

Automatically categorize transactions and reconcile accounts.

Detect anomalies or potential errors in financial data.

Develop predictive models for cash flow forecasting.

This enhanced capability can be a game-changer for accountants, allowing you to offer better insights and services to your clients.

The Quest for Efficiency

Efficiency is a prized asset in the world of accounting. By integrating Python into your accounting software, you're empowering yourself with a versatile toolkit to enhance data management, automate processes, and gain deeper insights.

With Python as your ally, data transfer and analysis are no longer daunting tasks but rather opportunities for innovation. The synergy between the adaptability of Python and the power of accounting software can lead to breakthroughs in productivity, accuracy, and client satisfaction.

Streamlined Accounting Operations

The integration of Python with accounting software represents a significant step forward in the evolution of accounting. The power to streamline data transfer, automate repetitive tasks, and perform advanced analysis is at your fingertips. Whether you're managing a small business or handling a complex portfolio of clients, the possibilities are endless. As we wrap up our exploration of advanced topics in Python for accounting, remember that the world of finance is in constant evolution. Staying informed and adapting your skills is essential to remain at the forefront of the industry. Always be open to emerging technologies and continue your journey through the ever-changing landscapes of accounting and Python.

Emerging Trends in Accounting Technology

In the ever-evolving landscape of accounting, the only constant is change. As you've embarked on this journey to master Python for accounting, it's essential not just to understand the current state of affairs but to also keep your sights firmly set on the emerging trends and technologies that are shaping the future of this profession. In this chapter, we will delve into the exciting realm of emerging trends in accounting technology and how Python is at the forefront of this transformative wave.

The field of accounting is no longer confined to number-crunching and ledger management. It's rapidly evolving into a dynamic and data-driven domain, and technology is at the heart of this transformation. Let's explore the key trends that are influencing the world of accounting.

1. Automation and Artificial Intelligence: Automation is already making waves in the accounting world. Routine tasks such as data entry, invoice processing, and even basic financial analysis are increasingly being automated. This not only saves time but also minimizes human errors. Python plays a pivotal role in this automation, with libraries like Pandas and NumPy driving data manipulation.

2. Cloud Accounting: With the advent of cloud computing, accountants can access data from anywhere, collaborate in real-time, and leverage the power of cloud-based applications. This not only streamlines accounting processes but also enhances data security. Python can be used to develop cloud-based applications and tools, allowing accountants to harness the benefits of the cloud.

3. Big Data Analytics: In the digital age, businesses are generating vast amounts of data. Accountants are now expected to derive meaningful insights from this data to support strategic decision-making. Python, with its robust data analytics libraries, enables accountants to process and analyze massive datasets efficiently.

4. Cybersecurity and Data Protection: With the increasing digitization of financial data, ensuring data security has become paramount. Cyber threats are ever-evolving, and accountants must be vigilant in safeguarding sensitive financial information. Python is instrumental in developing security tools to protect data and prevent breaches.

5. Blockchain Technology: Blockchain is revolutionizing how financial transactions are recorded and verified. Accountants are increasingly being called upon to understand and audit blockchain-based financial systems. Python can be used to develop smart contracts and applications on blockchain platforms.

6. Predictive Analytics: Accountants are no longer just historians; they are also futurists. Predictive analytics, driven by machine learning and Python, enables accountants to forecast financial trends and identify potential risks and opportunities.

7. Regulatory Technology (RegTech): Staying compliant with ever-changing regulations is a challenge for accountants. RegTech solutions, often powered by Python, automate compliance tasks and help accountants ensure that their organizations adhere to the latest regulatory requirements.

8. Data Visualization: As the volume of data accountants deal with continues to grow, effective data visualization is crucial. Tools like Matplotlib, coupled with Python, empower accountants to create informative and visually engaging financial reports and dashboards.

9. Remote Work and Collaboration: The rise of remote work necessitates collaborative tools for accountants. Python can be used to create custom applications that facilitate remote collaboration and data sharing securely.

Python is the glue that binds these trends together. Its versatility and vast ecosystem of libraries make it an ideal choice for accountants looking to stay ahead in this tech-driven era. As you explore these emerging trends, remember that Python is not just a programming language but a passport to the future of accounting.

By mastering Python and staying updated on the latest trends, you're positioning yourself as a forward-thinker and a valuable asset to any accounting team or organization. The Python skills you acquire through this book will not only equip you for the current challenges but also empower you to adapt and thrive in an ever-changing accounting landscape.

In the realm of financial analysis with Python, we've ventured deep into the heart of data-driven insights and predictive power.

You've learned how to harness Python's capabilities to dissect financial data, calculate ratios, and unveil meaningful trends. As we draw the curtains on this chapter, you're equipped with a valuable arsenal of analytical skills that are vital in the world of accounting.

In Chapter 6, "Regulatory Compliance and Security," we're diving into the core of safeguarding financial integrity and ensuring compliance with evolving regulations. You'll discover how Python can be your trusted companion in navigating the intricate landscape of data privacy, security, and regulatory requirements. Get ready to explore the critical aspects of maintaining the trust and integrity that underpins the financial world.

CHAPTER 6: REGULATORY COMPLIANCE AND SECURITY

In the world of finance and accounting, adherence to regulatory standards and the safeguarding of financial data are paramount. Chapter 6, "Regulatory Compliance and Security," delves into the critical aspects of this complex terrain. We will embark on a journey that explores the measures, practices, and technologies required to ensure data privacy, compliance with legal standards, and the protection of financial assets. This chapter equips you with the knowledge and tools to maintain the trust and integrity that are the cornerstones of the accounting profession. So, let's embark on this crucial exploration of regulatory compliance and security in the digital age.

Data Privacy and GDPR Compliance

In the modern landscape of accounting, data is the lifeblood of financial operations. Every transaction, every ledger entry, and every financial statement resides in the digital realm, making the protection of this data a critical responsibility. The importance of data privacy and compliance with regulations cannot be overstated, especially in the wake of the European Union's General Data Protection Regulation (GDPR).

Data Privacy: Safeguarding the Foundations

Data privacy goes beyond simply securing information from unauthorized access. It's about protecting the confidentiality, integrity, and availability of financial data. In the realm of accounting, ensuring the privacy of data is not only a legal requirement but also a trust-building measure with clients and stakeholders.

From confidential client records to financial statements, an accountant's work involves handling a wealth of sensitive information. Any breach of this data can have severe consequences, both legally and in terms of reputation. Therefore, it's imperative to implement stringent safeguards, including encryption, secure access controls, and regular security audits.

Python's versatility comes into play in establishing robust security measures. You can develop and implement encryption algorithms, secure authentication systems, and intrusion detection systems using Python, thus ensuring data privacy.

GDPR Compliance: Navigating the Regulatory Landscape

The introduction of GDPR in 2018 significantly impacted the way data is managed and protected. GDPR imposes strict regulations on the collection, storage, processing, and transfer of personal data. This regulation, while originating in the European Union, has a global reach as it applies to any organization handling EU citizens' data. Therefore, understanding and complying with GDPR is not optional; it's a necessity.

The GDPR places specific emphasis on data subjects' rights, ensuring that individuals have control over their personal data. For accountants, this means ensuring consent when collecting data, allowing data access to individuals, and providing the right to erasure (commonly known as the "right to be forgotten").

Python's capabilities extend to GDPR compliance through the development of data handling systems that allow individuals to access and control their data. It facilitates the creation of data audit trails and secure data erasure processes, addressing GDPR's core requirements.

Furthermore, the law mandates data protection impact assessments (DPIAs) for activities that might result in high risks to individuals' rights and freedoms. Python's data analysis capabilities prove invaluable in conducting DPIAs, helping accountants identify, assess, and mitigate data privacy risks.

The Role of Encryption: Python in Action

One of the fundamental aspects of ensuring data privacy is encryption. Encrypting sensitive financial data renders it unintelligible to unauthorized parties. Python offers a plethora of libraries and tools for implementing encryption effectively.

For example, the Cryptography library in Python provides a wide range of cryptographic recipes and capabilities, allowing you to encrypt data using various methods such as AES and RSA encryption. By leveraging this library, you can seamlessly integrate encryption into your accounting systems, ensuring that financial data is protected both at rest and during transmission.

Secure Access Controls: Limiting Data Exposure

Access control is another vital component of data privacy. It involves defining and managing who can access specific data and what actions they can perform. Python's simplicity and versatility make it an excellent choice for developing access control mechanisms.

You can create role-based access controls, ensuring that only authorized personnel can access particular financial data. Using Python's libraries and frameworks, you can develop secure login systems, access restriction mechanisms, and audit trails that help track who accessed what data and when.

Building Trust: Data Privacy as a Competitive Advantage

In the dynamic field of accounting, clients and stakeholders seek reliability, integrity, and security in their financial partners. Demonstrating a commitment to data privacy and GDPR compliance not only safeguards your practice from legal risks but also enhances your reputation.

Clients are increasingly scrutinizing how their financial data is handled. Being able to assure them that their information is protected and that you comply with international regulations like GDPR can give your practice a significant competitive edge.

In summary, the importance of data privacy and GDPR compliance in accounting cannot be understated. By leveraging Python's capabilities, accountants can build a robust security framework that ensures data privacy and meets the stringent demands of modern regulations. It's not just about compliance;

it's about trust, integrity, and securing the future of accounting in the digital age.

Now, as we delve further into Chapter 6, we will explore the realm of security best practices in accounting. We'll uncover the strategies, tools, and techniques that protect your financial data from cyber threats and vulnerabilities, ensuring that the foundations of trust remain unshaken. So, let's venture into the realm of security and fortify your accounting practices.

In accounting sensitive financial data flows like a river, the safeguarding of information is paramount. In the age of digitalization, this task becomes more challenging yet crucial. In this section, we dive into the realm of security best practices, ensuring the fortress around your financial data is impervious to potential cybersecurity threats.

In today's digital landscape, security is not just an option; it's a necessity. Cyber threats have become increasingly sophisticated, and they pose substantial risks to the financial world. Accounting firms and professionals deal with vast amounts of sensitive data, ranging from personal financial details to confidential corporate information. Hence, implementing security measures is non-negotiable.

Understanding the Perimeter:

Before we delve into the specific measures, let's understand the perimeter we're looking to secure. Your financial data exists in a variety of digital formats, from spreadsheets to databases, and it resides on servers, cloud storage, and local devices. Each of these can be a potential target for cyberattacks. Moreover, these threats come in various forms, including but not limited to:

Data Breaches: Unauthorized access to financial data, which can lead to identity theft, financial fraud, and reputational damage.

Ransomware Attacks: Malicious software that encrypts your data, rendering it inaccessible until a ransom is paid.

Phishing: Deceptive techniques used to acquire sensitive information, such as names, passwords, and credit card details.

Malware: Malicious software designed to disrupt, damage, or gain unauthorized access to computer systems.

Insider Threats: Risks posed by individuals within the organization who have access to confidential information.

Given this complex threat landscape, we must adopt a multi-faceted approach to protect our financial data.

Guarding the Vault:

Data Encryption: One of the fundamental strategies is data encryption. Ensure that all your financial data, whether it's stored on servers, in the cloud, or on local devices, is encrypted. This means that even if an unauthorized entity accesses it, the data will be indecipherable.

Access Control: Implement strict access controls. Only

authorized personnel should have access to financial data, and each access point should be monitored and controlled. Consider employing two-factor authentication for an extra layer of security.

Regular Updates and Patch Management: Cybersecurity threats often exploit vulnerabilities in outdated software. Regularly update and patch your operating systems, applications, and antivirus programs to fortify your defenses.

Firewalls and Intrusion Detection Systems: Employ firewalls and intrusion detection systems to monitor incoming and outgoing network traffic. These systems can alert you to suspicious activities and prevent unauthorized access.

Training and Awareness: Your team is your first line of defense. Conduct cybersecurity training to make everyone aware of best practices and potential threats. Encourage a culture of vigilance.

Cyber Hygiene:

Besides these basic security measures, it's essential to cultivate good cyber hygiene practices. Here are some additional tips:

Regular Backups: Frequently back up your financial data. If a cyber incident occurs, you'll still have access to your information.

Incident Response Plan: Develop a comprehensive incident response plan. This document should outline the steps to take in case of a security breach, minimizing damage and recovery time.

Penetration Testing: Regularly engage in penetration testing to identify vulnerabilities in your security systems. It's better to find and fix these issues before malicious actors can exploit them.

Data Classification: Categorize your financial data based on its sensitivity. Apply security measures in accordance with these classifications.

Security Audits: Periodically conduct security audits to assess the effectiveness of your security measures and ensure compliance with industry regulations.

Monitoring and Alerts: Implement real-time monitoring systems that can detect unusual activities and immediately alert your security team.

As you navigate the intricate web of accounting data, these security best practices will serve as your armor, protecting your financial information from the ever-evolving threats in the digital world.

Now, let's transition to the next section, where we explore the establishment of internal controls and audit trails. These practices are crucial in preventing financial fraud and errors while maintaining transparency and accountability within your accounting processes.

]

Internal Controls and Audit Trails

Maintaining the highest standards of accuracy and accountability is non-negotiable. As we delve into the intricate realm of internal controls and audit trails, you'll discover how Python can be a powerful ally in safeguarding your financial data.

The term "internal controls" might sound intimidating, but it's essentially a set of rules and procedures designed to ensure the integrity of financial transactions within an organization. It encompasses a series of checks and balances that deter fraud, prevent errors, and guarantee transparency in accounting practices. But how does Python fit into this equation? Let's explore this together.

Python for Internal Controls

Picture this: You're an accountant responsible for managing the financial records of a medium-sized company. Ensuring that every transaction is accurate and adheres to established standards is a Herculean task. This is where Python's automation capabilities come to the forefront.

Python allows you to create custom scripts and programs that can automatically validate financial data. For example, you can set up automated checks to ensure that no transaction exceeds a certain limit without proper authorization. Python can alert you when such transactions occur, saving you from hours of manual data scrutiny.

Additionally, Python can help in managing roles and permissions. You can assign specific roles to individuals within your organization, determining who can access, modify, or delete financial data. These role-based controls contribute to the prevention of unauthorized or fraudulent activities.

The Power of Audit Trails

Now, let's move on to the concept of audit trails. An audit trail is a chronological record of all activities related to a specific operation or transaction. It serves as a comprehensive history of changes, which can be crucial in identifying discrepancies or resolving disputes.

Python's ability to automate this process is invaluable. By incorporating Python scripts into your accounting software, you can generate detailed audit trails for every financial transaction. These logs include the who, what, when, and where of each operation. If an error or discrepancy occurs, you can easily trace back through the audit trail to identify when and where the issue originated.

The Python Advantage

Imagine a scenario where you detect an anomaly in your financial records. An unexpected alteration in an account balance has raised suspicion. With Python, you can trace the discrepancy back to its source. You can identify which made the change, when it occurred, and whether it was authorized or not. This level of transparency and accountability is what sets Python apart.

Now, let's put this into practice with a simple Python example.

We'll create a basic audit trail system to track changes to an account balance:

python

```python
import datetime

class Account:
    def __init__(self, account_id, initial_balance):
        self.account_id = account_id
        self.balance = initial_balance
        self.transaction_history =

    def deposit(self, amount):
        self.balance += amount
        self.transaction_history.append(f"Deposited    ${amount} on {datetime.datetime.now()}")

    def withdraw(self, amount):
        if self.balance >= amount:
            self.balance -= amount
            self.transaction_history.append(f"Withdrew        ${amount} on {datetime.datetime.now()}")
        else:
            print("Insufficient funds.")

# Let's create an account and perform some transactions
acc = Account(1, 1000)
acc.deposit(500)
```

```
acc.withdraw(200)

# Display the account balance and transaction history
print(f"Current Balance: ${acc.balance}")
print("Transaction History:")
for transaction in acc.transaction_history:
    print(transaction)
```

In this example, the Account class tracks deposits and withdrawals, storing them in a transaction_history list. Each transaction includes a timestamp. While this is a basic example, it illustrates how Python can be used to create an audit trail for financial operations.

By integrating such features into your accounting system, you can ensure transparency and accountability, making it far more challenging for errors or fraudulent activities to go unnoticed.

Internal controls and audit trails are like the guardians of your financial data. They work tirelessly to ensure the accuracy and reliability of your records. With Python, you have the tools to automate and streamline these processes, enhancing your ability to protect your organization from fraud, errors, and discrepancies.

As you journey through the realm of accounting, remember that Python is not just a programming language; it's a trusted ally in maintaining the highest standards of integrity in financial practices. So, embrace it, harness its capabilities, and continue to explore the incredible possibilities it offers in the world of accounting. Your commitment to transparency and accuracy will set you on a path to success in this dynamic field.

Legal Considerations

As an accountant integrating Python into your daily practices, understanding the legal landscape is paramount. Without a clear comprehension of the legal intricacies surrounding accounting and financial reporting, even the most meticulously prepared financial data can lead to troubles that are best avoided.

Understanding the Legal Framework

Before we delve into the specifics of Python's role in accounting, let's establish a foundation by discussing the broader legal framework. Financial reporting and accounting have always been subject to legal regulations. Compliance with these regulations is essential for maintaining transparency and trust in the financial world.

Laws and standards like the Generally Accepted Accounting Principles (GAAP) in the United States and the International Financial Reporting Standards (IFRS) worldwide dictate how financial data should be recorded and reported. Failure to adhere to these standards can result in severe legal consequences.

Python's Role in Ensuring Compliance

Python, with its powerful data manipulation and analysis capabilities, plays a pivotal role in helping accountants adhere to these standards. By integrating Python into your accounting practices, you can facilitate compliance through the following avenues:

Data Integrity: Python can be used to develop automated

data validation and integrity checks. This ensures that financial data entered into your systems meets legal standards. Any inconsistencies or anomalies can be flagged, preventing erroneous data from affecting financial reports.

Audit Trails: In this digital age, maintaining an audit trail is not only a best practice but often a legal requirement. Python scripts can be employed to establish comprehensive audit trails for every financial transaction. These trails provide a chronological history of all actions taken in your accounting systems, enhancing transparency and accountability.

Compliance Reporting: Python can streamline the process of preparing compliance reports. With the ability to manipulate and analyze vast datasets, Python can ensure that your financial statements meet the necessary legal standards. Furthermore, it can help in automating the generation of these reports, saving time and reducing the risk of human error.

Data Privacy and GDPR Compliance

Apart from traditional accounting standards, it's essential to consider the increasingly critical aspect of data privacy. The General Data Protection Regulation (GDPR) in the European Union has had a far-reaching impact on how financial data is handled, even outside the EU.

Python's versatility allows you to create tools that help in ensuring data privacy and GDPR compliance. From data anonymization to robust access control mechanisms, Python can be tailored to meet specific legal requirements.

Guarding Against Cybersecurity Threats

In this digital age, cybersecurity is a pressing concern for accountants. With the ever-looming threat of data breaches, protecting sensitive financial information is not just good practice; it's legally mandated in many jurisdictions. Python can be utilized to develop security measures that safeguard your financial data against potential cybersecurity threats.

The Importance of Compliance Management

The final section of this chapter,, examines a real-world case study that illustrates effective compliance management. This case study provides a practical insight into how Python can be leveraged to navigate complex legal requirements successfully. By understanding and applying these legal considerations, you can protect your organization from costly legal battles, maintain the trust of your stakeholders, and ensure the integrity of your financial reports.

Accounting and financial reporting are not merely about crunching numbers; they are also about ensuring compliance with a myriad of legal standards. Python, with its versatile capabilities, empowers accountants to meet these standards effectively. By integrating Python into your accounting practices, you can establish robust internal controls, maintain comprehensive audit trails, and streamline compliance reporting. This chapter serves as your guide to understanding the legal landscape and leveraging Python to thrive in the world of accounting, all while remaining on the right side of the law.

Legal Frameworks in Accounting:

Accounting operates within a structured legal framework, shaped by laws and regulations designed to maintain transparency, accountability, and integrity in financial reporting. One such regulation is the Generally Accepted Accounting Principles (GAAP) in the United States, which sets the standard for financial reporting. Other countries have their own standards, like the International Financial Reporting Standards (IFRS), followed by many nations. It's vital to comprehend these frameworks since Python can be a powerful tool for implementing them effectively.

Compliance with Financial Regulations:

Each nation, state, or jurisdiction may have its unique financial regulations. Compliance is crucial in preserving the legal integrity of financial data. Failing to adhere to these regulations can lead to severe consequences, including financial penalties, legal actions, and damage to an organization's reputation. Python can assist in automating compliance tasks, ensuring that every financial transaction adheres to the relevant laws and standards.

Data Privacy and GDPR:

One of the critical aspects of legal considerations in the digital age is data privacy. In the European Union, the General Data Protection Regulation (GDPR) imposes strict guidelines on the handling and protection of personal data. For accountants dealing with international clients or organizations, understanding GDPR is essential. Python's data manipulation capabilities can be harnessed to ensure compliance with GDPR requirements, such as anonymizing data or implementing data protection impact assessments.

Anti-Money Laundering (AML) and Know Your Customer (KYC):

Financial institutions, including banks and investment firms, are mandated to follow Anti-Money Laundering (AML) and Know Your Customer (KYC) regulations. These regulations are intended to prevent money laundering, fraud, and the financing of illegal activities. Python can be a valuable tool in streamlining AML and KYC processes, making compliance more efficient and effective.

Case Study: Handling Compliance

To illustrate how Python can aid in effective compliance management, let's consider a case study of a financial institution that needs to ensure adherence to AML and KYC regulations.

In this scenario, the institution implements a Python-based solution to automate the customer due diligence process. This system collects, validates, and cross-references customer data with government-sanctioned watchlists and databases. Python's libraries for data extraction, manipulation, and validation simplify this process, allowing for efficient and accurate customer assessments.

Moreover, the institution uses Python to establish an audit trail, ensuring the traceability of every transaction and customer interaction. In the case of an audit, Python's capabilities make it easier to provide a comprehensive record of all actions taken and decisions made regarding compliance.

The case study highlights how Python can streamline compliance management, making it not only more efficient but also more thorough and accurate. By leveraging Python's automation capabilities, the financial institution ensures that they remain on the right side of the law, avoiding hefty penalties and safeguarding their reputation.

Best Practices for Managing Regulatory Compliance:

Stay Informed: Regulatory landscapes change, so make

sure you're up-to-date with the latest legal requirements and guidelines.

Leverage Technology: Implement Python-based solutions to automate compliance tasks, reducing human error and ensuring thoroughness.

Audit Trails: Maintain a comprehensive audit trail to provide transparency and accountability in compliance efforts.

Regular Training: Ensure that your team is well-versed in the legal requirements and the Python tools used for compliance.

Documentation: Keep thorough records of compliance efforts and actions taken.

Legal considerations in accounting are not to be taken lightly. Incorporating Python can be a game-changer in compliance management, offering efficiency and accuracy in navigating the complex regulatory landscape. The case study provided demonstrates that Python is not just a tool for data analysis but also an essential asset for maintaining compliance. As the financial world continues to evolve, the ability to effectively manage compliance is more critical than ever, and Python is at the forefront of that endeavor.

Conclusion

In Chapter 6, we've delved into the crucial realm of regulatory compliance and security in accounting, highlighting the significance of adhering to legal standards and safeguarding sensitive financial data. We've explored the tools and practices that Python offers to enhance compliance management, from automating due diligence to maintaining comprehensive audit trails.

As we embark on the next leg of our journey, Chapter 7:

"Case Studies and Practical Applications," we will take the knowledge gained in compliance and security and apply it in real-world scenarios. These case studies will demonstrate how Python empowers accountants and financial professionals to make sound decisions, prevent fraud, optimize investments, and ensure efficient tax planning. Prepare to witness Python in action as we tackle practical challenges and unveil the true potential of this dynamic tool in accounting. Join us in Chapter 7 for inspiring case studies and practical applications that bring theory to life.

CHAPTER 7:
CASE STUDIES
AND PRACTICAL
APPLICATIONS

In accounting, we encounter one of the most pressing issues in financial management - fraud detection. It's a topic that carries substantial weight in the accounting profession, and rightly so. In an era where data flows at an unprecedented pace and volume, ensuring the integrity of financial data and protecting it from fraudulent activities is paramount. In this chapter, we will embark on a journey to explore how Python can be harnessed to identify, prevent, and combat financial fraud effectively.

Understanding the Need for Fraud Detection

Financial fraud, ranging from embezzlement to sophisticated cybercrimes, can have devastating consequences for businesses, stakeholders, and the economy as a whole. As accountants, it is our responsibility to maintain the trust and integrity of financial systems. But where do we start?

Python as the Sherlock Holmes of Accounting

Python, often hailed as the versatile programming language, becomes our trusted ally in this quest. Its powerful data analysis capabilities, extensive libraries, and machine learning modules equip us with the tools to detect anomalies, uncover irregularities, and preempt financial crimes. While many may see accountants as number crunchers, we now wield the power to be the ultimate detectives.

The Data Landscape of Fraud Detection

Before we jump into Python code and fraud detection techniques, let's get acquainted with the data landscape. In the modern accounting world, data is scattered across various platforms and systems. Financial transactions occur online, through mobile devices, and legacy systems. This complex ecosystem serves as a playground for fraudsters.

Data sources may include transaction logs, customer records, employee information, and market data. With Python, we can aggregate, clean, and preprocess this data efficiently.

Anomaly Detection - The Key to Unmasking Fraud

In the realm of fraud detection, the emphasis is on identifying anomalies. Anomalies are data points that deviate significantly from the expected pattern. For example, detecting an unusually high transaction amount for a customer who typically makes smaller purchases is a potential anomaly.

Python libraries like Scikit-Learn provide various anomaly detection algorithms, including Isolation Forests and One-Class SVM. These algorithms can be applied to uncover suspicious activities in large datasets.

python

```python
# Example code for Isolation Forest anomaly detection
from sklearn.ensemble import IsolationForest

# Create an Isolation Forest model
model = IsolationForest(contamination=0.05)

# Fit the model to your data
model.fit(data)

# Predict anomalies
anomalies = model.predict(data)
```

Machine Learning for Fraud Classification

Beyond anomaly detection, Python enables us to implement machine learning models for fraud classification. These models can categorize transactions or activities as 'fraudulent' or 'legitimate'. Machine learning algorithms like Random Forest, Logistic Regression, and Neural Networks can be utilized for this purpose.

python

```python
# Example code for building a Random Forest classifier
from sklearn.ensemble import RandomForestClassifier

# Create a Random Forest model
model = RandomForestClassifier()
```

```
# Train the model on labeled data
model.fit(X_train, y_train)

# Predict fraud on new data
fraud_predictions = model.predict(X_test)
```

Real-World Application - Case Studies

Theory becomes more tangible when applied to real-world scenarios. In this chapter, we will dissect case studies that showcase how Python can be employed for fraud detection. These studies will walk you through practical situations, from transactional fraud in e-commerce to internal employee fraud.

The case studies will involve data preprocessing, model selection, training, and evaluation. It's essential to understand that there's no one-size-fits-all solution in fraud detection. The approach varies based on the nature of your business and the data at hand.

Constant Vigilance - The Need for Continuous Monitoring

Fraud detection isn't a one-time endeavor. The digital landscape evolves, and with it, fraudsters develop new techniques. Python can assist in setting up automated systems that continuously monitor transactions and data, flagging potential fraud in real-time.

Incorporating historical fraud data, machine learning models can adapt and improve their accuracy over time. This continuous monitoring and learning is an essential aspect of a comprehensive fraud detection strategy.

As we conclude our exploration of fraud detection with Python, remember that being proactive in identifying and preventing fraud is a cornerstone of ethical accounting practices. Python empowers accountants to act as vigilant guardians of financial integrity.

Through the application of machine learning, data analysis, and continuous monitoring, you can become the Sherlock Holmes of your financial institution, uncovering clues hidden within the data. By identifying and preventing fraud, you not only protect your organization's financial health but also contribute to the broader economic stability.

Case Study: Investment Portfolio Analysis

Managing investment portfolios is akin to steering a ship through ever-changing waters. Just as a seasoned captain relies on navigational tools, investors need the right tools and strategies to make informed decisions. In this case study, we'll delve into the realm of investment portfolio analysis using Python, shedding light on how this versatile programming language can be your trusted co-captain in your financial journey.

Understanding Investment Portfolio Analysis

To embark on our journey, let's first understand what investment portfolio analysis entails. Investment portfolios are collections of assets, such as stocks, bonds, real estate, or even cryptocurrencies, carefully chosen to balance risk and return. Analyzing these portfolios involves evaluating their performance, risk exposure, and composition.

Python, with its powerful libraries and data analysis capabilities, provides a comprehensive toolkit for performing such analyses. From calculating returns and risks to optimizing asset allocations, Python allows investors to make data-driven decisions.

Measuring Portfolio Performance

One of the primary objectives in investment portfolio analysis is measuring portfolio performance. Investors are interested in understanding how their investments are faring. Python's mathematical libraries, such as NumPy and Pandas, come into play here. These libraries provide efficient ways to calculate important performance metrics.

Python Example:

python

```
import numpy as np
import pandas as pd
import yfinance as yf # Yahoo Finance library for data retrieval

# Define a list of stock symbols
assets =

# Retrieve historical stock price data
data    =    yf.download(assets,    start='2020-01-01',
end='2022-01-01')

# Calculate daily returns
```

```
returns = data.pct_change().dropna()

# Calculate portfolio returns and risk
weights =   # Assuming equal allocation
portfolio_returns = np.dot(returns, weights)
portfolio_std_dev        =        np.sqrt(np.dot(weights,
np.dot(returns.cov(), weights)))
```

The example above demonstrates how you can use Python to retrieve historical stock price data, calculate daily returns, and compute portfolio returns and risk. These metrics are essential for gauging the performance of your investments.

Optimizing Asset Allocations

Efficient portfolio management involves optimizing asset allocations to achieve desired financial goals while managing risk. Python's libraries are instrumental in this regard. The SciPy library, for instance, offers optimization functions to help investors find the most efficient allocation.

Python Example:

python

```
from scipy.optimize import minimize

# Define a function to minimize negative portfolio returns
(maximize returns)
def portfolio_performance(weights, returns):
    portfolio_returns = np.dot(returns, weights)
```

```
    return -portfolio_returns

# Define constraints: sum of weights equals 1, and each weight
between 0 and 1

constraints  =  ({'type':  'eq',  'fun':  lambda  weights:
np.sum(weights) - 1},

        {'type': 'ineq', 'fun': lambda weights: weights})

# Define bounds for asset weights (0 to 1)
bounds = tuple((0, 1) for asset in range(len(assets)))

# Initial guess for weights (equal allocation)
initial_guess =

# Run the optimization
optimized_weights   =   minimize(portfolio_performance,
initial_guess, method='SLSQP',

             bounds=bounds, constraints=constraints)

# Optimal weights for maximizing returns
optimal_allocation = optimized_weights.x
```

In the example, we use Python to optimize asset allocations by maximizing portfolio returns, considering constraints and bounds. This process helps investors make data-informed decisions regarding their investments.

Assessing Risk and Diversification

Another vital aspect of investment portfolio analysis is risk assessment and diversification. Python libraries offer tools to analyze the risk associated with different assets and how they interact within a portfolio.

Python Example:

python

```
# Calculate portfolio risk (standard deviation) and correlation matrix
portfolio_std_dev = np.sqrt(np.dot(optimal_allocation, np.dot(returns.cov(), optimal_allocation)))
correlation_matrix = returns.corr()

# Visualize risk and correlation
import matplotlib.pyplot as plt

plt.figure(figsize=(8, 6))
plt.scatter(portfolio_std_dev, portfolio_returns, c='g', marker='o')
plt.title('Portfolio Risk vs. Return')
plt.xlabel('Portfolio Risk (Standard Deviation)')
plt.ylabel('Portfolio Return')
plt.grid(True)
```

In this snippet, we use Python to calculate the portfolio's standard deviation (risk) and create a correlation matrix. Visualizing risk versus return provides insights into the diversification benefits of your portfolio.

Risk Mitigation and Strategy

Python offers opportunities to implement risk mitigation strategies, such as stop-loss orders and asset rebalancing. By incorporating these strategies into your investment portfolio analysis, you can protect your investments and ensure they align with your financial goals.

In conclusion, Python is not merely a programming language but a financial companion for investors. It equips them with the tools and knowledge needed to navigate the complexities of investment portfolio analysis. In this ever-evolving financial landscape, Python's flexibility and analytical prowess empower investors to make informed decisions, optimize returns, and mitigate risks, ensuring a smoother and more prosperous journey towards financial success.

Remember, the examples provided here are just a glimpse of what Python can do in investment portfolio analysis. The possibilities are vast, and your journey into Python-assisted investing is filled with opportunities for exploration and growth.

Case Study: Tax Planning

In this section, we delve into a critical aspect of financial management - tax planning. Tax planning is an essential part of financial decision-making, as it can significantly impact an organization's or individual's financial health. Leveraging Python for tax planning offers numerous advantages, from optimizing tax efficiency to ensuring compliance with tax regulations. This case study will explore the intricacies of using Python in tax planning and how it can help you make informed decisions regarding your financial obligations.

Maximizing Tax Efficiency with Python

Tax planning involves minimizing your tax liability by making strategic financial decisions. Python provides a versatile toolkit for analyzing financial data, which is crucial for tax planning. By harnessing Python's data analysis capabilities, you can gain insights into your financial situation, income sources, and expenditures. These insights empower you to make informed decisions about deductions, exemptions, and credits that can reduce your tax burden.

Let's consider an example. Suppose you are a small business owner. Python can help you analyze your income and expenses, identify potential deductions, and optimize your tax strategy. With data at your fingertips, you can make educated decisions about the timing of income and expenses to maximize deductions and minimize taxable income.

Python for Tax Modeling

Tax planning often involves creating models to simulate different financial scenarios and their tax implications. Python excels in this domain as well. With libraries like Pandas, NumPy, and Matplotlib, you can build comprehensive financial models to assess how various factors impact your tax liability.

Imagine you're planning to invest in a new project. Python allows you to create financial models that project the potential income, expenses, and tax implications. By changing variables in the model, such as revenue projections or capital investments, you can instantly see how these modifications affect your tax position. This enables you to make strategic financial decisions to minimize taxes while achieving your financial goals.

Real-time Tax Updates and Compliance

Tax laws are subject to change, and keeping up with the latest regulations is vital for accurate tax planning. Python can be used to automate the process of monitoring tax law changes. By integrating your financial data with real-time tax law APIs or web scraping tools, you can receive instant updates on changes that may affect your tax planning. This ensures that you remain compliant and can adapt your financial strategy accordingly.

For example, if a new tax incentive or credit becomes available, your Python-based system can alert you to its potential benefits. This way, you can take advantage of any new tax breaks that apply to your situation.

Case Study Example

Let's walk through a hypothetical case study. Suppose you're a self-employed individual running a freelance business. You want to optimize your tax planning strategy for the upcoming year. With Python, you can:

Analyze your income and expenses from the previous year.

Identify potential deductions, credits, and exemptions.

Create a tax model that considers different scenarios.

Monitor tax law changes throughout the year.

Make informed decisions regarding your financial actions to maximize tax efficiency.

By following these steps and utilizing Python for your tax planning, you can potentially save a significant amount of money and reduce the stress associated with tax season.

Python Code Example: Tax Deduction Optimization

Here's a simplified Python code snippet to illustrate how you can use Python for tax deduction optimization:

python

```
import pandas as pd

# Sample income and expenses data
income =
expenses =

# Calculate total income and expenses
total_income = sum(income)
total_expenses = sum(expenses)

# Calculate taxable income
taxable_income = total_income - total_expenses

# Define tax deductions
standard_deduction = 12000
deductions = 0

# Check if itemized deductions exceed standard deduction
if sum(expenses) > standard_deduction:
    deductions = sum(expenses)

# Calculate total deductions
```

```python
total_deductions = standard_deduction if deductions < standard_deduction else deductions

# Calculate taxable income after deductions
taxable_income_after_deductions = taxable_income - total_deductions

print("Total Income: $", total_income)
print("Total Deductions: $", total_deductions)
print("Taxable Income: $", taxable_income_after_deductions)
```

In this example, the code calculates taxable income after considering deductions. You can customize it with your financial data to analyze your own tax situation.

Tax planning is an integral part of financial management. Python offers a powerful platform to assist individuals and businesses in optimizing their tax strategies. By harnessing its data analysis and modeling capabilities, you can make informed financial decisions, respond to tax law changes, and maximize your tax efficiency.

Real-World Applications and Success Stories

Adaptability and innovation are key to staying ahead. As you've delved into the realms of Python for accounting, you've learned not just a new programming language but a powerful tool that can transform the way financial tasks are managed and executed. In this chapter, we'll explore real-world success stories and applications of Python in accounting. These are the tales of professionals and organizations who embraced this dynamic duo and reaped the rewards. By the end of this chapter, you'll not only be informed but also inspired to chart your own journey towards Python-driven accounting excellence.

Python in the Corporate Landscape

Across various industries and businesses, Python has been heralded as a game-changer, but it's particularly notable in the corporate sector. Many organizations have realized the potential of Python for financial management, reporting, and analysis.

Case 1: A Multinational Corporation

Consider a multinational corporation with a vast network of subsidiaries. Managing financial data and ensuring consistency across diverse regions was a challenge. They adopted Python to automate the consolidation of financial statements, eliminating errors and saving countless hours of manual work. Through Python scripts, they achieved real-time financial data synchronization, enhancing decision-making and reducing risks.

Case 2: A Financial Services Firm

In the world of financial services, timely data analysis is a competitive advantage. A financial services firm integrated Python into their operations, streamlining data collection and processing for investment portfolios. With Python's power in data visualization, they provided their clients with interactive dashboards and real-time market insights. This not only improved client relationships but also boosted their reputation as a tech-savvy and innovative firm.

Enhancing Efficiency and Accuracy

Case 3: Tax Consultancy

Tax regulations are complex and ever-evolving. A tax consultancy firm faced challenges in keeping up with tax law changes and ensuring their clients' compliance. They utilized Python to build a tax compliance tool. This tool automatically updated with the latest tax codes and provided precise tax planning recommendations. With Python's ability to process vast amounts of data swiftly, they improved accuracy and efficiency, helping their clients make informed decisions.

Case 4: Small Business Accounting

It's not just the big players who benefit from Python. Consider a small accounting firm catering to local businesses. They used Python to automate repetitive tasks like invoicing, payroll, and expense tracking. This allowed them to focus on providing more personalized financial advice to their clients. Moreover, they adopted Python for data visualization, making it easier for their clients to understand their financial reports.

Startups and Python Prowess

Case 5: A Tech Startup

Startups, often constrained by limited resources, find Python to be a versatile and cost-effective solution. A tech startup used Python to develop a financial forecasting model, leveraging machine learning. They were able to secure investor funding by showcasing how Python could predict financial trends with greater accuracy, making their business more attractive to potential backers.

Case 6: A Blockchain Accounting Startup

With the rise of blockchain technology, a new niche has emerged. Blockchain accounting is a specialized field dealing with cryptocurrencies and digital assets. A startup harnessed Python's capabilities to create an accounting platform for cryptocurrency transactions. Their Python-based solution made it easier to trace and account for various cryptocurrency transactions while ensuring compliance with tax regulations.

Bridging the Gap: Python and Accounting Education

Python's influence isn't limited to the corporate world. Educational institutions and online platforms have recognized its importance in training the next generation of accountants and financial analysts.

Case 7: Accounting Academics

Leading universities have integrated Python into their accounting programs. Professors teach students how to use Python for financial analysis and reporting. These students, armed with Python proficiency, enter the workforce as highly sought-after professionals, driving change within the industry.

Success Beyond Measure

These success stories underscore Python's role as a transformative force in accounting. Whether you're part of a multinational corporation or a one-person accounting firm, Python can be tailored to suit your needs. It's not just a tool but a gateway to efficiency, accuracy, and innovation in the world of finance.

With every line of code and every analysis run, Python opens new possibilities and uncovers insights. The journey you've embarked on in this book has the potential to lead you to uncharted territories. As you venture further, keep these stories in mind. They are a testament to the boundless potential of Python for accountants. Now, it's your turn to script your success story.

Conclusion

So far, we've traversed a landscape teeming with innovation and real-world success stories. From corporate giants to nimble startups, Python has made its indomitable mark on financial management, reporting, and analysis. Through automation, data visualization, and predictive modeling, it has transformed the way financial professionals operate.

These case studies provide tangible proof of Python's ability to enhance efficiency, accuracy, and competitiveness. No matter the scale or sector of your financial operations, Python can be tailored to optimize your processes and decision-making.

As you conclude this chapter, remember that the world of accounting is evolving, and Python is your bridge to the future. Whether you're embarking on a career in accounting, guiding your business through financial intricacies, or seeking innovative solutions for your clients, Python is your companion on this journey.

These case studies are not just tales of success; they are your roadmap to realizing the boundless potential of Python in accounting. With each Python script you write, with each data analysis you perform, you're taking a step towards a future where efficiency, accuracy, and innovation reign supreme in the world of finance.

So, let these practical applications be your inspiration, your proof that Python isn't just a language; it's a gateway to financial excellence. Now, with these stories in your arsenal, step confidently into the future, embracing the endless possibilities Python brings to the world of accounting.

CHAPTER 8: BEST PRACTICES AND TIPS - INTRODUCTION

As you've progressed through the world of Python for accounting, you've acquired the knowledge, skills, and insights needed to harness the power of this versatile language in financial tasks. Now, as we delve into Chapter 8, we shift our focus towards mastering the art of using Python efficiently and effectively.

This chapter serves as a compass guiding you through the best practices, essential strategies, and valuable tips that can elevate your Python proficiency to new heights. Here, you'll discover the core principles of writing well-structured and documented Python code, fostering effective collaboration, and staying at the forefront of an ever-evolving field.

Just as a skilled conductor orchestrates a symphony, your understanding of best practices and tips will allow you to harmonize Python's capabilities with your accounting objectives. You'll uncover the secrets of maintaining clear, readable code, facilitating teamwork through version control, and leveraging the wealth of resources available in the Python community.

The financial world is one of precision and accuracy, and this chapter equips you with the tools to uphold these principles in your Python endeavors. It is not just about writing code; it's about crafting solutions that are efficient, maintainable, and collaborative.

Why is this chapter so crucial, you might ask? Well, think of your code as the backbone of your accounting solutions. It needs to be robust, reliable, and understandable, not just for you but for your team members and potential collaborators. In this section, we're going to guide you through the best practices that will elevate your coding game and ensure that your Python scripts are a joy to work with.

Writing Well-Structured Code: The Blueprint of Success

Imagine constructing a sturdy building. You need a well-thought-out blueprint that outlines every detail, from the foundation to the roof. In Python, your code's structure serves as that blueprint. A well-structured script is easier to read, maintain, and expand. But what makes code "well-structured"?

Firstly, break down your code into functions. Each function should have a specific purpose, making it easier to understand what that section of code is doing. For instance, if you're working on a financial analysis script, consider having separate functions for data loading, data analysis, and reporting. This modular approach enhances code reusability and maintainability.

Clear and Meaningful Variable Names: The Language of Code

Code should be self-documenting. This means that when someone reads your code, they should be able to understand its purpose without having to consult external documentation. The key to achieving this is using clear and meaningful variable names.

Let's consider a practical example:

python

```
# Poor Variable Naming
a = 10
b = 5
result = a * b

# Improved Variable Naming
income = 10
expenses = 5
profit = income * expenses
```

Which one is more readable and easier to comprehend? Meaningful variable names are a cornerstone of clean code.

Documentation: Your Code's Compass

Documentation is your code's compass. It guides you and others through the intricacies of your Python script. While Python is renowned for its readability, adding comments and docstrings to explain the "why" and "how" of your code is a best practice.

For instance, consider the following piece of code:

python

```
# Calculate the average profit margin
def calculate_profit_margin(total_profit, total_revenue):
    """
    This function calculates the profit margin.

    :param total_profit: Total profit
    :param total_revenue: Total revenue
    :return: Profit margin as a percentage
    """
    profit_margin = (total_profit / total_revenue) * 100
    return profit_margin
```

Here, the docstring explains what the function does, what parameters it expects, and what it returns. This is incredibly helpful for anyone who might collaborate on your project or even for yourself when you revisit the code after a few months.

Consistency and Style Guides: The Roadmap to Clarity

Python has established style guides, such as PEP 8, that dictate naming conventions, indentation, and other aspects of code style. Adhering to these guidelines ensures that your code is consistent and easy to understand.

For instance, PEP 8 suggests using snake_case for variable and function names, maintaining a consistent indentation of four spaces, and adhering to a maximum line length of 79 characters. These rules might seem small, but they significantly enhance the readability and maintainability of your codebase.

Let's look at how this works in practice:

python

```
# Inconsistent Code
totalProfit = 10000
total_revenue = 25000
def calculateProfitMargin(totalProfit, total_revenue):
    return (totalProfit / total_revenue) * 100

# Consistent Code (PEP 8)
total_profit = 10000
total_revenue = 25000

def calculate_profit_margin(total_profit, total_revenue):
    return (total_profit / total_revenue) * 100
```

In the consistent code, it's immediately evident that the variables and function names follow the snake_case convention, and the indentation is consistent. This small adjustment makes a big difference.

In addition to PEP 8, there are linters and code formatters, such as flake8 and black, that can automatically enforce these guidelines. Integrating these tools into your development process can save you time and maintain code consistency.

Now that you've uncovered the fundamental aspects of writing clean, well-structured code, it's time to apply these principles to your Python projects. The goal is to make your code a masterpiece of clarity and maintainability. In the next chapter, we'll explore strategies for collaborative coding and version control, another critical aspect of successful Python accounting projects.

The Power of Collaboration

In the world of accounting, projects often involve multiple stakeholders with distinct roles and responsibilities. Effective collaboration is the cornerstone of success. When it comes to coding, this means working closely with your colleagues, accountants, and financial analysts to ensure the project aligns with the desired outcomes. Collaboration isn't just about sharing the workload; it's about leveraging diverse skills to create something exceptional.

To foster successful collaboration, consider the following strategies:

1. Define Roles and Responsibilities

Clear communication is essential from the outset. Define the roles of team members, outlining who is responsible for what. This minimizes misunderstandings and ensures everyone knows their part in the project.

2. Version Control with Git

Version control systems like Git are invaluable for tracking changes to your code and documents. Git allows multiple team members to work on the same project simultaneously, and it keeps a detailed history of changes. GitHub and GitLab are popular platforms that integrate Git for online collaboration.

3. Consistent Coding Standards

Adopting consistent coding standards is essential when working with others. A clear, agreed-upon coding style ensures that everyone can understand and work on the codebase efficiently. PEP 8, Python's style guide, is a great reference for maintaining a uniform coding style.

4. Effective Communication

A project's success relies heavily on effective communication. Whether it's through regular meetings, chat apps like Slack, or emails, open channels of communication are crucial for addressing concerns and tracking progress.

Version Control with Git

Let's delve deeper into the power of version control, particularly with Git, which has become the industry standard. Git allows you to track and manage changes in your code efficiently. It's a distributed version control system, which means that every developer has a local copy of the entire project history.

Understanding Git Terminology

Before we get into the practical side of things, let's understand some fundamental Git terminology:

Repository (Repo): This is your project directory. It contains all the files, history, and configuration.

Commit: A commit represents a snapshot of your repository at a specific point in time. Each commit has a unique identifier.

Branch: A branch is a separate line of development. You can create branches to work on features or fixes independently.

Clone: Cloning means creating a copy of a repository on your local machine.

Pull: Pulling refers to fetching changes from a remote repository and merging them into your current branch.

Push: Pushing is the process of sending your commits to a remote repository.

Collaborative Workflow

When collaborating with others using Git, consider the following workflow:

Clone the Repository: Start by cloning the central repository to your local machine. This gives you a local copy to work on.

Create a Branch: Before working on a new feature or bug fix, create a new branch. This keeps your work isolated from the main project until it's ready to merge.

Make Commits: Work on your branch and make commits as you go. Each commit should represent a logical and self-contained change.

Pull and Merge: Regularly pull changes from the main repository to stay up to date. If there are conflicts, resolve them before continuing.

Push Your Branch: When your feature or fix is complete, push your branch to the remote repository. This makes your changes available to others.

Create a Pull Request: If you're working on a project like GitHub, create a pull request to propose your changes. This allows others to review your code and discuss any potential modifications.

Review and Merge: Collaborators review your pull request. Once it's approved, your code can be merged into the main branch.

Remember that effective collaboration isn't just about sharing code but also about sharing knowledge and insights. Respect your team's ideas and experiences, and you'll build a stronger and more effective project together.

Tools for Efficient Collaboration

Collaboration doesn't stop at workflows and communication; it also involves tools that streamline the process. Here are some valuable tools for efficient collaboration in the world of Python programming for accountants:

1. GitHub and GitLab

These platforms provide an online space to host, manage, and collaborate on Git repositories. They offer features like issue tracking, pull requests, and project management boards.

2. Slack

Slack is a popular team collaboration tool that simplifies communication through channels, direct messaging, and integrations with various services.

3. JIRA

JIRA is a robust project management tool by Atlassian. It's excellent for tracking project progress, managing issues, and coordinating tasks.

4. Trello

Trello is a simple, visual project management tool that uses boards, lists, and cards to organize tasks and facilitate collaboration.

5. Google Workspace

Google Workspace provides a suite of cloud-based tools like Google Docs, Sheets, and Drive for real-time collaboration on documents and data.

6. Zoom

For video conferences, webinars, and screen sharing, Zoom is a widely used platform that brings teams together regardless of their locations.

The world of Python programming for accountants is dynamic, and collaboration is the key to staying on top of it. By defining roles, maintaining coding standards, and using version control effectively, you can ensure your projects run smoothly. Remember, collaboration isn't just about sharing code; it's about sharing knowledge, experiences, and the joy of learning together. Collaborate efficiently, and you'll excel in the world of Python accounting.

Harnessing the Power of Collaboration

Efficiency in teamwork can make all the difference when it comes to tackling complex projects or resolving intricate accounting problems. In this digital age, collaborative coding is not just an option; it's a necessity. This section will guide you on how to harness the power of collaboration using Python.

In the realm of Python for accounting, where projects often involve multiple team members, you'll find that collaborating on code is indispensable. No longer is software development the solitary pursuit it once was. Today, collaboration is the name of the game. Python's versatility and adaptability make it an excellent choice for collaborative projects.

Strategies for Efficient Teamwork

This section provides insights into strategies for efficient teamwork in Python for accounting. The integration of Python in accounting practices has given rise to multidisciplinary teams where accountants, data analysts, and programmers work together to achieve common goals.

Effective teamwork begins with a clear division of tasks and roles. In Python projects, responsibilities may be distributed among team members, with each individual having specific roles and expectations. This structured approach ensures that everyone is aware of their responsibilities and can work harmoniously toward the project's objectives.

Project Management in Accounting

Good project management is a cornerstone of successful Python implementations in accounting. As projects grow in complexity, the need for effective project management becomes increasingly evident. This section will discuss the significance of managing projects efficiently and how it contributes to the success of Python for accounting endeavors.

Accounting projects can vary widely in scope and scale, from simple data analysis tasks to complex financial forecasting models. Effective project management enables teams to set clear objectives, establish timelines, allocate resources, and track progress. In Python for accounting, this can be the difference between smooth execution and chaotic development.

Version Control: A Must for Collaboration

This section emphasizes the critical importance of version control systems in collaborative Python projects for accounting. Version control systems are like the guardians of your codebase. They provide a structured approach to managing code changes, tracking revisions, and preventing conflicts among team members.

Version control systems allow team members to work on different aspects of a project simultaneously. These systems also help in tracing changes, locating bugs, and ensuring that all code versions are neatly organized. Whether you are working on an accounting report automation tool or a financial forecasting model, version control makes it easier to work together and deliver high-quality results.

Leveraging Git for Collaborative Python Projects

Git is one of the most widely used version control systems in the world of programming. In this section, we'll explore how Git can be harnessed for managing Python projects in accounting. With Git, you can track changes, collaborate with others, and contribute to projects without interfering with each other's work.

Git's distributed nature allows team members to work independently and merge their work seamlessly. It simplifies the process of identifying and resolving conflicts in the codebase. For accountants stepping into the realm of Python, Git is a versatile tool that ensures their collaboration with developers is productive and hassle-free.

Problem-Solving through Online Communities and Forums

In the world of Python for accounting, the learning journey is continuous. As you embark on your path to mastering Python, you may encounter roadblocks and challenges along the way. This is where the support of online communities and forums can be invaluable.

There's a wealth of Python enthusiasts and experts willing to lend a helping hand when you're facing programming puzzles or accounting conundrums. In this section, we'll explore the vast ecosystem of online Python communities and forums, where you can ask questions, seek advice, and share your experiences. By tapping into these resources, you can enhance your problem-solving skills and benefit from the collective wisdom of the Python community.

Staying Updated with Evolving Technologies

Python is a dynamic language, and the world of accounting is constantly evolving. Therefore, it's essential to stay updated with the latest trends and technologies. In this section, we'll discuss the importance of continuous learning and skill development in Python for accounting.

The world of accounting is increasingly relying on data-driven insights, and Python is at the forefront of this evolution. By staying informed about emerging technologies and trends, you can position yourself as a forward-thinker in the accounting profession. This section will provide strategies and resources to help you keep your skills up to date.

Collaboration and version control are not mere buzzwords in the Python for accounting landscape; they are essential components of successful projects. Embracing efficient teamwork, robust project management, and version control systems can elevate your Python endeavors in the field of accounting. By leveraging the power of online communities and continuously learning and adapting to changes, you can stay at the forefront of the ever-evolving accounting profession. In this chapter, you'll discover that the synergy between collaboration, version control, and continuous learning is the key to unlocking the full potential of Python in accounting.

The Need for Lifelong Learning

As a Python enthusiast in the world of accounting, you've already taken a significant step towards embracing technology. Python is a versatile and powerful tool, and it's continuously enhanced by a thriving community of developers. However, your journey doesn't end with this book. To truly excel in your career and keep pace with the latest developments, you must commit to lifelong learning.

Technology evolves at a breakneck speed, and with it, so does the field of accounting. Regulatory changes, new software tools, and emerging best practices all demand your attention. Continuous learning isn't just about acquiring new skills; it's also about adapting to industry trends and staying ahead of the curve.

Resources for Lifelong Learning

Thankfully, the digital age has brought an abundance of resources right to your fingertips. The following are some key avenues to explore:

1. Online Courses and Tutorials: Platforms like Coursera, edX, and Udemy offer a vast array of courses, from Python programming to advanced accounting techniques. These courses often allow you to learn at your own pace, making it easy to integrate with your work.

2. Professional Organizations: Joining accounting and data analysis professional organizations is a fantastic way to access valuable resources. These organizations often provide webinars, articles, and networking opportunities.

3. Blogs and Forums: Stay active in online communities and forums related to both Python and accounting. Websites like Stack Overflow, Reddit's r/learnpython, and the Python community forums are excellent places to ask questions and learn from experienced practitioners.

4. Conferences and Meetups: Attending conferences, both virtual and in-person, is a great way to learn about the latest trends in the field. These events often feature experts who share their knowledge and insights.

5. Books and Publications: Just as you're doing now, reading books and publications is an excellent way to deepen your knowledge. Industry-specific publications and Python-related books can provide in-depth information on specialized topics.

Strategies for Continuous Learning

Acquiring new skills is one thing, but integrating learning into your routine is another. Here are some strategies to help you make learning a regular part of your professional life:

1. Set Clear Goals: Define what you want to learn and achieve in your career. Setting clear goals will help you focus your learning efforts.

2. Allocate Time: Dedicate a specific portion of your schedule to learning. Whether it's a few hours each week or a more intensive learning session, consistency is key.

3. Keep a Learning Journal: Maintain a journal to track your progress, jot down new insights, and reflect on how your learning is impacting your work.

4. Seek Feedback: Don't hesitate to seek feedback from peers, mentors, or online communities. Constructive criticism can be a powerful tool for growth.

5. Collaborate and Share: Engaging with peers and sharing your knowledge can reinforce your learning. Teaching others can be a powerful way to consolidate your understanding.

6. Stay Inquisitive: Curiosity is your ally. Keep asking questions, even if they seem basic. The pursuit of knowledge often begins with a simple query.

7. Explore New Technologies: Python is just one piece of the puzzle. Stay open to exploring new technologies and tools that

can complement your Python skills.

Embracing the Future

As you venture forward, remember that the skills and knowledge you acquire today will serve as the foundation for the innovations of tomorrow. It's a journey of perpetual growth and discovery. So, as you close this chapter on continuous learning and skill development, set your sights on the ever-advancing horizons of Python in accounting, and step forward with curiosity, determination, and an unwavering commitment to self-improvement. The future is yours to shape.

Preparing for Future Changes

The world of accounting, much like the ever-evolving realm of technology, is in a constant state of transformation. As professionals, accountants are required to adapt to these changes and embrace the innovative tools and techniques that can enhance their practices. In this chapter, we delve into the strategies and mindsets needed to prepare for the future and stay ahead in the field of accounting, leveraging the power of Python.

Adaptation and Agility

Accountants who adapt quickly and efficiently to change position themselves for success. In the realm of accounting, change can take various forms, from regulatory updates and new compliance standards to emerging technologies. The first step in preparing for the future is to cultivate agility. Much like the Python programming language itself, accountants must be flexible, responsive, and open to new ideas and practices.

Consider a scenario where a significant change in financial reporting regulations is introduced. An agile accountant recognizes the need for adjustments in their methodologies, systems, and reporting formats. With the flexibility to quickly pivot and implement these changes, they can ensure compliance and provide valuable insights to their clients or organizations.

However, agility alone is not sufficient. To thrive in the face of change, accountants must also embrace technology.

Embracing Technology

The digital age has revolutionized the accounting landscape, with automation, data analytics, and artificial intelligence becoming integral to the profession. Python, with its versatility and vast library ecosystem, has emerged as a powerful tool for accountants. As a future-focused accountant, it's crucial to not only use existing technologies but also to stay updated with emerging trends.

One of the best strategies for future-proofing your accounting career is to invest time in continuous learning. Whether you're already proficient with Python or a novice, staying informed about the latest developments is paramount. Engage in online courses, attend webinars, or participate in workshops to deepen your understanding and harness the full potential of Python.

Incorporating Python's machine learning capabilities into your skill set can be a game-changer. This empowers you to provide more accurate financial forecasts, identify patterns and trends, and automate tedious tasks, thereby increasing efficiency. Moreover, as artificial intelligence and machine learning continue to advance, a solid foundation in Python opens the door to harnessing these technologies for even more profound insights.

Strategies for Staying Ahead

Now, let's explore specific strategies to prepare for future changes effectively:

Stay Informed: Keep abreast of developments in both the accounting and technology fields. Subscribe to relevant journals, follow industry experts on social media, and join professional organizations that offer insights into emerging trends.

Networking: Actively participate in accounting communities and engage in discussions about the latest trends and best practices. Networking can also open doors to collaboration on projects involving Python and accounting.

Coding Skills: Enhance your Python skills continually. While not every accountant needs to be a professional coder, understanding Python is a significant advantage. As the language evolves, so should your knowledge.

Adopt Automation: Implement automation tools for routine accounting tasks. These tools can reduce errors, enhance efficiency, and free up time for more strategic activities.

Data Analysis: Deepen your data analysis capabilities. Python's libraries like Pandas can help you unlock valuable insights from financial data, enabling better-informed decision-making.

Security Awareness: With data breaches becoming more common, understanding cybersecurity is vital. Ensure that you stay informed about the latest cybersecurity threats and the best practices for safeguarding financial data.

Adaptive Mindset: Foster a mindset of adaptability. The future is uncertain, but your ability to embrace change and innovate will help you thrive, not just survive.

Python for accounting is not just a skill; it's an enabler for accountants to flourish in a dynamic environment. By developing the skills and strategies outlined in this chapter, you can confidently stride into the future of accounting, equipped to face challenges and seize opportunities with Python as your trusted companion.

And as the field of accounting continues to evolve, remember that the journey is just as important as the destination. Your passion for learning and commitment to staying ahead in the ever-changing world of accounting with Python will lead to a fulfilling and successful career.

Preparing for future changes in accounting and technology involves embracing agility, continuously learning, and harnessing the potential of Python. With the right mindset and a commitment to innovation, you can navigate the complexities of the modern accounting landscape and find yourself well-prepared for whatever the future holds. Stay agile, stay informed, and let your Python journey in accounting propel you into a world of exciting possibilities.

Conclusion: Looking Ahead

In the ever-evolving landscape of accounting and technology, we've explored the strategies and skills needed to prepare for the future. By embracing agility, harnessing the power of Python, and fostering a mindset of adaptability, you are now better equipped to navigate the dynamic world of accounting. As we conclude this chapter, remember that your commitment to innovation and continuous learning is your ticket to a flourishing career in the field of accounting.

As we venture into the next chapter, we'll address the common mistakes in Python programming that accountants should avoid. We'll also delve into potential pitfalls in accounting practices and discuss strategies for maintaining data integrity and upholding ethical standards. By recognizing these challenges and being prepared to tackle them, you can further enhance your skills and ensure the success of your Python-powered accounting journey. So, let's dive into Chapter 9 and explore the nuances of overcoming these hurdles as a Python-savvy accountant.

CHAPTER 9:
CHALLENGES
AND PITFALLS

Welcome to Chapter 9 of "Python for Accounting." In the previous chapters, we've journeyed through the foundations of Python, data handling, financial analysis, automation, and best practices. As you've honed your skills and embraced the opportunities that Python offers, it's time to confront the challenges and pitfalls that await accountants in this digital age.

This chapter is dedicated to helping you navigate the potential roadblocks and obstacles you might encounter along the way. From common mistakes in Python programming to the intricacies of data integrity, ethical considerations, and staying updated with ever-changing regulations, we'll provide you with the knowledge and strategies to overcome these challenges. By understanding the potential pitfalls and having the tools to avoid them, you'll ensure that your journey through Python for accounting is a smooth and successful one. So, let's dive in and equip ourselves with the wisdom to tackle these hurdles head-on.

Common Mistakes in Python Programming

As you continue your journey in mastering Python for accounting, it's important to be aware of the common pitfalls and programming errors that can trip up even the most seasoned developers. In this section, we'll delve into the most frequent mistakes encountered in Python programming and equip you with the knowledge to identify and avoid them. The ability to steer clear of these blunders will not only enhance your code quality but also ensure the reliability of your Python applications.

Let's begin by exploring some of the common mistakes that aspiring Python programmers often make:

1. Ignoring Proper Indentation:

Python relies on indentation for code structure. Failing to indent code correctly can lead to syntax errors, making your code unreadable and unmanageable. Let's take a simple example:

python

```
if x > 5:
print("x is greater than 5") # Incorrect indentation
```

To avoid this mistake, ensure that all indents are consistent throughout your code.

2. Uninitialized Variables:

Variables used without prior initialization can lead to unpredictable behavior in your Python programs. For instance:

python

```
amount = amount + 5  # 'amount' is used before initialization
```

Make sure to initialize variables before using them to prevent such errors.

3. Confusing Assignment Operators:

Python has various assignment operators, such as '=' for assignment and '==' for comparison. Mixing them up can lead to unintended consequences:

python

```python
if x = 5:  # Should be 'if x == 5:'
    print("x is equal to 5")
```

Always use the correct operator to avoid this mistake.

4. Forgetting to Close Files:

When working with files, forgetting to close them after use can lead to resource leaks and even data corruption. Here's an example:

python

```python
file = open("data.txt", "r")
# Perform file operations
# Missing 'file.close()' statement
```

Remember to close files explicitly with the close() method or use a with statement to ensure proper handling.

5. Not Handling Exceptions:

Ignoring exceptions and errors in your code can result in unexpected program crashes. It's crucial to implement exception handling, as shown here:

python

```python
try:
    result = num1 / num2  # 'num2' should not be zero
except ZeroDivisionError:
    print("Division by zero is not allowed")
```

Catch and handle exceptions to provide a graceful response to errors.

6. Poor Variable Naming:

Choosing unclear or non-descriptive variable names can make your code difficult to understand. Consider this example:

python

```python
x = 5  # What does 'x' represent?
```

Opt for meaningful variable names that convey their purpose.

7. Lack of Comments and Documentation:

Failing to document your code with comments and docstrings can make it challenging for others (or even your future self) to understand and maintain. Remember to include explanations and docstrings to clarify your code's functionality.

Now that we've explored these common programming mistakes, let's discuss how to avoid them and enhance your Python code quality.

Avoiding Common Mistakes and Improving Code Quality

To steer clear of the pitfalls mentioned above, follow these best practices:

Adhere to Python's Indentation Rules: Ensure consistent and proper indentation. This not only maintains readability but also prevents syntax errors.

Initialize Variables: Always initialize variables before using them to avoid unpredictable behavior.

Use Clear Assignment Operators: Differentiate between assignment and comparison operators to prevent errors in conditions and assignments.

Close Files: Properly close files after usage, either by using the close() method or a with statement.

Implement Exception Handling: Handle exceptions gracefully to prevent program crashes and provide meaningful error messages.

Choose Descriptive Variable Names: Opt for variable names that clearly convey their purpose and improve code readability.

Include Comments and Documentation: Document your code with comments and docstrings to aid understanding and maintainability.

By being mindful of these common mistakes and applying these best practices, you'll significantly enhance your Python programming skills and produce code that is more robust, reliable, and maintainable. In the world of accounting, where precision is paramount, mastering these aspects of Python programming is crucial for success.

Identifying the Landmines

One of the most prevalent pitfalls in accounting is the mishandling of data. Often, accountants are faced with vast amounts of financial information, and a simple error during data entry can result in significant issues down the line. Be it a misplaced decimal point or a typo in an account number, these seemingly minor mistakes can snowball into massive discrepancies. To avoid these landmines, accountants need to be vigilant and double-check their entries. Here's where Python comes to the rescue.

Mitigating Errors with Python

Python offers a powerful set of tools to help accountants manage and validate their data efficiently. Whether it's data cleansing, validation, or complex calculations, Python can be a reliable partner in ensuring data accuracy.

Data Cleansing: Python provides libraries like Pandas that are designed to clean and preprocess data. It can help accountants eliminate duplicate entries, handle missing values, and ensure that data is consistent and accurate.

Automated Validation: Writing Python scripts to validate data can be a game-changer. Accountants can set up rules and conditions to flag entries that fall outside acceptable parameters. For instance, Python scripts can be used to check whether expenses exceed a certain threshold or if income sources match declared values.

Integration with Accounting Software: Python can seamlessly integrate with existing accounting software. This means that data can be automatically cross-checked and validated, reducing the risk of human error in data entry.

Taxing Troubles

Tax season is an annual ordeal that many dread. The complexity of tax laws and the constant changes in regulations can lead to a minefield of potential errors. Some common issues include incorrect filing statuses, failure to claim valid deductions and credits, or errors in calculations.

Python can play a significant role in tackling these challenges. Accountants can use Python to:

Automate Tax Calculations: By creating scripts that perform tax calculations based on the latest tax codes and regulations, Python can help ensure that tax returns are accurate.

Cross-Check Deductions: Python can be programmed to cross-reference deductions and credits with the taxpayer's information, minimizing the risk of missing out on potential savings.

Provide Real-Time Updates: Python can pull real-time tax information and updates from government websites, ensuring that the tax returns are always up-to-date with the latest regulations.

Ethical Evasion

Ethics is at the core of accounting, and any deviation can lead to professional and financial consequences. Sometimes, the line between ethical and unethical practices can be blurry. For instance, shifting losses between accounts to reduce tax liability is considered unethical. Python can help accountants maintain transparency and ethical practices.

Audit Trails: Python scripts can be implemented to create comprehensive audit trails, ensuring that any financial activity is tracked and documented. This not only helps with transparency but also acts as a deterrent against unethical practices.

Detecting Anomalies: Python can identify anomalies or unusual patterns in financial data that might indicate unethical activities. This includes identifying suspicious transactions or accounting practices.

Steering Clear of Fraud

Accounting fraud is a severe issue that can result in significant financial losses and even legal consequences. Some common types of fraud include embezzlement, misreporting financial statements, or inflating revenues. Python can be a valuable asset in fraud prevention.

Continuous Monitoring: Python can be programmed to monitor financial data continuously. It can flag unusual patterns that might indicate fraudulent activities, such as unexpected spikes in revenue or dubious expense claims.

Advanced Analytics: Python's data analytics capabilities are incredibly valuable in identifying fraud. It can analyze data sets to discover hidden patterns that might indicate fraudulent behavior.

In accounting, vigilance is essential. The ability to recognize and mitigate common accounting pitfalls can save not only money but also a company's reputation. By leveraging Python's capabilities in data validation, tax calculations, ethics adherence, and fraud prevention, accountants can ensure that their work is both accurate and ethically sound. Remember, in accounting, precision and ethics are two sides of the same coin.

The Foundation of Data Integrity:

Before we dive into the world of data validation, it's crucial to understand that data integrity begins with the way you collect, input, and handle your data. Ensuring accuracy right from the start can save you from a multitude of problems down the line. Even though Python is a powerful tool, it can only work with the data it's given. Garbage in, garbage out. Therefore, let's first explore the foundational steps for maintaining data integrity.

1. Data Collection and Input:

Accurate data starts with careful and meticulous collection. Ensure that the data sources you use are reliable and reputable. Whether you're dealing with financial transactions, client information, or market data, verify the authenticity and accuracy of your sources.

When inputting data, double-check for typographical errors, especially when manually entering information into your systems. A small typo can lead to significant discrepancies. Python's capabilities can help automate data input, but human oversight remains crucial.

2. Data Storage and Security:

Protecting data from unauthorized access and loss is another key aspect of data integrity. Use secure storage methods and implement access controls. Data breaches can result in tampered data, leading to distorted financial reports.

Ensure data backups are regular and comprehensive. In the event of a system failure or data corruption, a backup can be a lifesaver in maintaining data integrity.

3. Data Quality Assurance:

Regular data quality checks are essential. Create routines and automated scripts in Python to perform data validation, checking for missing values, inconsistencies, and outliers. For instance, you can use libraries like Pandas to detect and handle anomalies in your data.

Now, let's focus on data validation and the role Python plays in ensuring data integrity.

Data Validation with Python:

Python offers a wide array of tools and libraries to perform data validation effectively. These techniques are not only time-efficient but also reduce the likelihood of human errors.

1. Type Validation:

Ensure that data types match the expected format. For instance, if you're dealing with financial data, make sure that numerical values are indeed numbers and not strings. Python's type-checking functions can help validate the data's correctness.

Here's a simple Python code snippet for type validation:

python

```python
def is_number(value):
    try:
        float(value)
        return True
    except ValueError:
        return False
```

2. Range and Constraint Validation:

In financial analysis, many values must fall within specific ranges or adhere to certain constraints. Python allows you to set up rules and checks to ensure data falls within these boundaries. For instance, validating that an interest rate is between 0 and 1.

python

```python
def is_valid_interest_rate(rate):
    if 0 <= rate <= 1:
        return True
    else:
        return False
```

3. Cross-Field Validation:

Cross-field validation checks relationships between different data points. This is common when working with accounting data. For example, the sum of expenses should never exceed the total revenue.

Python code can be used to set up these cross-field checks:

python

```python
def is_balanced(revenue, expenses):
    if revenue >= expenses:
        return True
    else:
        return False
```

4. Referential Integrity:

Referential integrity validation ensures that data references are accurate. This is particularly important when dealing with databases. Python, along with database systems, allows you to set up foreign key constraints to enforce referential integrity.

For instance, in a database, you can link transactions to specific accounts. A Python script can verify that these links are valid.

5. Automated Validation Scripts:

To streamline data validation, you can create Python scripts that automatically run data checks. These scripts can be scheduled to run regularly, ensuring that data integrity is continuously maintained.

Preventing Costly Errors:

By implementing robust data integrity and validation practices, you can safeguard your financial analyses against costly errors. Python, with its vast libraries and automation capabilities, provides a powerful toolset for maintaining data accuracy.

Remember, data validation is not a one-time task but an ongoing process. The world of finance and accounting is dynamic, and your data must reflect these changes accurately. Whether you're an accountant or a financial analyst, Python's data validation capabilities will prove invaluable in your quest for precision and reliability.

Ethical Concerns

Ethical considerations in the world of accounting are of paramount importance. They form the bedrock upon which trust and integrity are built, and this holds true whether you're crunching numbers the old-fashioned way or leveraging the power of Python for your accounting tasks. In this section, we'll delve into the ethical responsibilities accountants face in an era driven by technology and data analytics.

Accounting is more than just a field of numbers; it's about people's livelihoods, businesses, and, ultimately, the trust of stakeholders. Ethical concerns in accounting are numerous, and as technology becomes increasingly integrated into the industry, new ethical challenges arise.

Transparency and Honesty

At the heart of ethical concerns in accounting is the need for transparency and honesty. No matter how advanced the tools you use, the core principles of accounting remain the same. You are responsible for maintaining accurate and truthful financial records. Whether it's a ledger book or a Python program, the commitment to maintaining this transparency should be unwavering.

When we talk about transparency, we also need to consider the responsibility to disclose potential conflicts of interest. This becomes critical when, for example, you're providing accounting services to multiple clients. It's imperative to be honest about any conflicts and handle them professionally.

Data Privacy and Security

With the advent of technology, especially when using Python to work with sensitive financial data, the need for safeguarding data privacy and security is more significant than ever. Ethical concerns related to data privacy revolve around ensuring that you handle data with care, respect privacy regulations, and protect it from unauthorized access.

Ethical accountants should strive to stay updated with the latest data privacy laws and regulations. This may include GDPR,

HIPAA, or other industry-specific standards. You have a moral duty to ensure that the financial data you handle is protected from breaches and misuse.

Professional Independence

Professional independence is a cornerstone of ethical accounting practices. When using Python for accounting, there can be instances where you rely on automation and AI for decision-making processes. In such cases, maintaining your professional judgment and independence is crucial.

You should be wary of any technology or software that compromises your ability to make independent decisions. While technology can assist you in making informed choices, the final call should remain yours. Independence of judgment ensures that your advice and actions are not influenced by any external parties.

Confidentiality

Confidentiality is another ethical concern that remains timeless. It is your responsibility to maintain the confidentiality of your clients' financial data, regardless of how you manage it. This principle should guide your practices, whether you're working with paper documents or sophisticated Python scripts.

This ethical concern extends to discussing cases or sharing sensitive data with colleagues. You must be discreet and only share information with authorized personnel. In the realm of technology, it's also essential to ensure the security of the systems you're using.

Social Responsibility

In the digital age, accountants must also consider their role in society. Ethical concerns related to social responsibility include analyzing the broader impact of financial decisions. Are the choices you're making in line with the best interests of society? Are they contributing positively to economic development and societal well-being?

Python, with its powerful data analysis capabilities, can help accountants examine the implications of various financial decisions. Ethical accountants should not only assess the ethical implications of individual transactions but also consider the societal consequences of financial activities and advice.

Avoiding Conflicts of Interest

In the rapidly evolving world of accounting technology, conflicts of interest can be more subtle. For instance, you may be tempted to recommend a certain software or solution because it benefits you personally, even if it's not the best choice for your client.

Ethical accounting demands that you identify, disclose, and address such conflicts promptly. Your primary responsibility is to your clients' interests, and any suggestion or decision should prioritize their needs above all.

In this era of technological transformation, the ethical landscape of accounting is continually shifting. The tools we use have evolved, but the fundamental principles of transparency, honesty, data privacy, and professional independence remain constant.

Upholding ethical standards in financial analysis and decision-making is not just a legal requirement; it's the moral obligation of every accountant. Regardless of the tools at your disposal, the responsibility to act ethically rests with you.

As you navigate the intersection of technology and ethics in accounting, remember that each action you take contributes to the overall trustworthiness of the profession. Python, when harnessed with ethical integrity, can be a powerful force for good in the world of accounting, helping you make sound financial decisions while upholding the highest ethical standards.

Now, let's move forward and explore the ethical challenges that accountants face in staying updated and adapting to changes in the accounting industry. It's a dynamic field that continually demands ethical vigilance and adaptation.

Keeping Abreast of Technological Advancements

The accounting landscape is constantly being reshaped by technological advancements. New software, tools, and platforms are introduced regularly, revolutionizing how accountants and financial professionals operate. Being in the know about these technological developments can provide a significant advantage in your career. Here are some strategies to ensure you remain updated:

1. Continuous Learning: The learning process doesn't stop once you've mastered the fundamentals of Python for accounting. It's essential to engage in continuous learning by enrolling in courses, webinars, or workshops that focus on the latest technologies and trends in accounting. Many online platforms offer courses in emerging technologies and accounting practices.

2. Professional Associations: Joining accounting and technology-related professional associations can be immensely beneficial. These organizations often provide resources, events, and networking opportunities that keep you informed about the latest industry trends and best practices. Associations like the AICPA (American Institute of Certified Public Accountants) and ISACA (Information Systems Audit and Control Association) are great places to start.

3. Technology News Sources: Regularly reading technology and accounting news sources, such as websites, blogs, or industry journals, can provide valuable insights into emerging trends and breakthroughs. By staying informed about the latest advancements in technology, you can anticipate how they might impact accounting.

4. Webinars and Conferences: Attending webinars and conferences is an excellent way to get firsthand knowledge from experts in the field. These events often cover cutting-edge technologies and offer a platform for discussing their practical applications in accounting.

Adapting to Regulatory Changes

In the world of accounting, regulatory changes are a constant. New laws, standards, and guidelines can significantly impact how financial data is managed, reported, and analyzed. It's crucial to not only understand these changes but also adapt your practices accordingly. Here's how to effectively manage regulatory changes:

1. Regulatory Monitoring: Stay vigilant about regulatory changes by regularly monitoring updates from relevant

government bodies and industry associations. For example, in the United States, the Financial Accounting Standards Board (FASB) often issues updates to Generally Accepted Accounting Principles (GAAP).

2. Compliance Workshops: Attending compliance workshops or training sessions can help you understand and implement new regulations effectively. These workshops are often conducted by experts and focus on the practical aspects of compliance.

3. Software Updates: Keep your software and tools up to date to ensure compliance with the latest accounting standards. Accounting software vendors frequently release updates to align with changing regulations.

4. Collaboration: Work closely with colleagues, compliance officers, or professionals who specialize in regulatory compliance. Collaborative discussions can be instrumental in adapting to new rules and standards.

Embracing Change and Innovation

Adapting to changes in technology and regulations requires an open mindset and a willingness to embrace innovation. Instead of fearing change, consider it an opportunity for growth and improvement. Here are some guiding principles:

1. Experimentation: Don't be afraid to experiment with new tools and technologies. Trial and error can be a valuable learning experience, and it's often through experimentation that you discover innovative solutions to accounting challenges.

2. Embrace Automation: As automation continues to shape the accounting field, welcome it as an ally, not a threat. Automating

routine tasks can free up time for more strategic and value-added activities.

3. Cross-Disciplinary Knowledge: Explore knowledge from related fields, such as data science and computer programming. These disciplines can offer fresh perspectives and approaches to accounting challenges.

4. Networking: Establish a strong professional network. Surrounding yourself with peers who are also committed to learning and adapting can be a powerful motivator.

Python, with its versatility and adaptability, will continue to be your faithful companion on this journey. The skills you've acquired throughout this book, combined with your commitment to staying updated and adapting to change, will position you as a leader in the ever-evolving world of accounting and technology.

So, dear reader, as you embark on your ongoing discoverywith Python in accounting, I encourage you to explore the uncharted territories of innovation, to embrace the winds of change, and to reach new heights in your accounting career. The future holds endless possibilities, and you, armed with knowledge and a commitment to adaptability, are well-prepared to seize them.

Conclusion

In conclusion, Chapter 9 has shed light on the paramount importance of staying updated with technology and adapting to changes in the accounting industry. We've explored strategies for continuous learning, keeping abreast of technological advancements, and effectively managing regulatory changes. Embracing innovation and maintaining a growth mindset are key takeaways as we prepare for the future. As we advance into the final chapter of this journey, remember that staying updated and adapting to change are not just skills but enduring principles in the ever-evolving world of accounting and technology.

CHAPTER 10: CONCLUSION AND BEYOND

As we reach the concluding chapter of our journey through the world of Python for accounting, it's time to reflect on the essential concepts and key takeaways that have been presented throughout this book. This chapter serves as a compass, guiding you back through the terrain we've covered and reinforcing the core knowledge you've acquired. So, let's embark on this reflective journey and summarize the key takeaways that will undoubtedly shape your understanding of Python for accounting.

A Recap of the Python Landscape:

In this book, we've navigated through the vast landscape of Python's applications in the field of accounting. From the foundational understanding of Python's syntax and variables to advanced topics like machine learning, natural language processing, and blockchain, you've gained a comprehensive view of what Python can offer to accountants.

Empowering Your Accounting Toolkit:

Python is not just a programming language; it's a powerful

tool that can enhance your efficiency and effectiveness as an accountant. By learning Python, you've added a versatile instrument to your toolkit, capable of automating repetitive tasks, performing complex financial analyses, and even delving into emerging fields like cryptocurrency accounting. The world of accounting is changing, and Python equips you to stay ahead of the curve.

Financial Analysis and Decision-Making:

You've explored how Python can aid in financial analysis and decision-making. Whether it's calculating financial ratios, performing time series analysis, or evaluating performance metrics, Python offers the means to make informed choices. By applying Python in your financial analyses, you'll gain a deeper understanding of your organization's financial health.

Data Handling and Visualization:

The ability to handle, clean, and visualize data is a crucial skill in the modern accounting landscape. Python's libraries like Pandas and Matplotlib empower you to wrangle data effectively and create meaningful visualizations. These tools have the potential to revolutionize your data-driven decision-making processes.

Automation and Efficiency:

Automation is the key to streamlining your accounting tasks. You've learned how to design Python scripts for handling data entry, reporting, and creating audit trails. These skills not only save you time but also enhance data integrity and accountability, vital aspects in today's financial world.

Ethical Considerations:

Ethical standards are of paramount importance in the field of accounting. You've explored the ethical aspects of handling financial data and the need to uphold ethical practices. Python can assist you in maintaining the integrity of financial data and ensuring compliance with legal requirements.

Staying Updated and Adapting:

The chapter you're currently reading emphasizes the importance of staying updated with technology and accounting regulations. The world of accounting and technology is ever-evolving. To stay relevant and competitive, it's crucial to continuously update your skills, adapt to changes, and embrace emerging trends.

Summary and Key Takeaways:

In this book, you've embarked on a comprehensive journey that has equipped you with the knowledge and skills to harness Python in the realm of accounting. As you reflect on the key takeaways, remember that Python is not just a language; it's your partner in enhancing efficiency, making informed financial decisions, and upholding ethical standards.

Reinforcing the core concepts and takeaways from this book, you'll carry forward a powerful tool that can revolutionize your accounting practices. Python's potential is vast, and it's up to you to explore its applications, dive into practical case studies, and embrace the future with enthusiasm.

The Ongoing Journey with Python in Accounting:

As you close this chapter and this book, I encourage you to see this as the beginning of a lifelong journey. Python's applications in accounting are continuously expanding. Embrace this journey, explore the possibilities, and remain curious. The world of Python is dynamic, and your skills can continue to evolve alongside it.

Final Thoughts and Encouragement:

In these pages, you've witnessed the fusion of technology and accounting, and I hope you're inspired by the potential it holds. The future of accounting belongs to those who adapt, learn, and remain passionate about their craft. Python can be your faithful companion on this journey, propelling you forward in the ever-changing world of accounting.

So, take the knowledge you've gained here, apply it with enthusiasm, and never stop exploring the boundless horizons that Python for accounting has to offer. Your journey has only just begun, and the future is waiting to be written with code, data, and innovation. May it be a journey filled with success, growth, and continuous learning.

ADDITIONAL RESOURCES

In your quest to master Python for accounting, this section provides a curated list of additional resources. Whether you're looking for further reading, online courses, or Python-related communities, these references will aid you in your ongoing journey to become a proficient Python-using accountant.

Books:

1. "Python for Data Analysis" by Wes McKinney - An essential reference for mastering Pandas, a crucial library in the Python accounting toolkit.

2. "Python for Finance" by Yves Hilpisch - This book is a valuable asset for anyone interested in Python's applications in the financial world.

3. "Automate the Boring Stuff with Python" by Al Sweigart - A fantastic resource for learning how to automate repetitive tasks with Python.

Online Courses:

1. Coursera - "Python for Everybody" - Offered by the University of Michigan, this course is a great starting point for Python beginners.

2. Udemy - "Python for Financial Analysis and Algorithmic Trading" - Learn how to use Python for financial analysis and algorithmic trading.

3. edX - "Data Science MicroMasters" - A series of courses

from top universities to master data science skills, including Python.

Websites and Forums:

1. Stack Overflow - A community of programmers where you can ask and answer Python-related questions.
2. Python.org - The official Python website for documentation and tutorials.
3. Reddit - r/learnpython - A subreddit for beginners to discuss and seek help on Python.

Financial Datasets:

1. Yahoo Finance - Access financial data for analysis.
2. World Bank Open Data - A rich source of global economic data for analysis.

IDEs and Tools:

1. PyCharm - A popular integrated development environment (IDE) for Python.
2. Jupyter Notebook - An open-source web application that allows you to create and share documents that contain live code, equations, visualizations, and narrative text.

Python Libraries:

1. Pandas - Official website for Pandas documentation and tutorials.
2. NumPy - Official website for NumPy documentation and tutorials.
3. Matplotlib - Official website for Matplotlib documentation and tutorials.

Certifications:

1. Certified Public Accountant (CPA) - The CPA credential is a fundamental certification for accountants.

2. Certified Management Accountant (CMA) - The CMA certification is highly regarded in management accounting.

Remember, the world of Python is vast and constantly evolving. This list is a starting point, and as you delve deeper into specific areas of Python for accounting, you'll discover more specialized resources. Keep learning, stay curious, and continue exploring the limitless possibilities that Python offers in the field of accounting. Your journey has just begun.

www.ingramcontent.com/pod-product-compliance
Lightning Source LLC
Chambersburg PA
CBHW071243050326
40690CB00011B/2236